WORDS FROM THE WEB:
Poems, Quotes, and Stories of Grief

The content associated with this book is the sole work and responsibility of the author. Gatekeeper Press had no involvement in the generation of this content.

Words From the Web:
Poems, Quotes, and Stories of Grief: I am a widow... this is my web.

Published by Gatekeeper Press
7853 Gunn Hwy., Suite 209
Tampa, FL 33626
www.GatekeeperPress.com

The editorial work for this book are entirely the product of the author. Gatekeeper Press did not participate in and is not responsible for any aspect of that element.

Library of Congress Control Number: 2023947702

ISBN (paperback): 9781662945267
eISBN: 9781662945274

WORDS FROM THE WEB:
Poems, Quotes, and Stories of Grief

I am a widow...
this is my web.
Eden Rule

gatekeeper press
Tampa, Florida

I dedicate this book to my four beautiful children who are my purpose in life;
they are the reason I got out of bed on most days over these past three years.
They give me meaning, joy, and show me that there is still something to live for.
Annie, Rosalan, Mark, and Lizzie –
I love you more than I can put into words. I am so honored to be your mother.

In honor and memory of my amazing husband, my best friend, my soul mate, my hero... my sweet Caleb.
I love you more than love. Hand in hand, heart to heart, forever.

Grief never ends...but it changes.
It's a passage, not a place to stay.
Grief is not a sign of weakness, nor a lack of faith,
it is the price of love.

On the hardest days, I remind myself that my grief is so harsh and catastrophic,
because the love was so powerful and special, and not everyone gets a love like that.

-Author unknown

Grief /gref/ *noun,* meaning deep sorrow, especially that caused by someone's death; the emotional suffering you feel when something or someone you love is taken away.

The definition makes it sound so simple, so explainable, so understandable. There are dozens of books and websites, therapy groups, camps, retreats, and counselors within reach to explain and help you understand grief, but one thing I have learned is this - grief is not simple, not explainable, not understandable.

There are no "stages of grief." The books and counseling community will say there are, theorists and psychologists will explain them to you, but there are no real stages of grief. A stage implies that you take steps in a linear path, moving from one place in grief to the next, and eventually reach the end; however, grief is not linear. There are steps you take throughout grief, but they go up and down, and down and up, and side to side, and back and forth, and repeat, and skip, and repeat, and continue...you never truly reach an ending stage. There is no set pattern, not for everyone and not even within each person. Each grief journey is unique as each love story is unique. There are no stages capable of containing all the experiences of love and grief's pain. Grief has no timeline; it is unending. Grief is not a race; it has no finish line. Grief has its own lifespan, unique to you. There is no time when pain and grief are completed. You grieve because you love, and love is a part of you. Love changes but does not end. Therefore, grief changes but does not end.

What will happen and what can happen, as you allow your grief, is that you will move differently with pain. It shifts and changes – sometimes heavy, sometimes light. Anger will happen. So will fear, peace, joy, guilt, confusion, and a range of other things. You will flash back and forth through many feelings, often several of them at once. Sometimes you will be tired of grief. You will turn away. And you'll turn back. And you'll turn away. And you'll turn back. Grief has a rhythm of its own – an unsteady heartbeat, an ebb and flow, a tide of waves, a roar.

Grief can make you feel like you are losing your mind. This does not mean that you are losing your mind. You will find yourself crazed within the crazy waves of grief, but you are not crazy. Grief is abnormally normal, and every crazed moment is normal.

There is no "closure." Grief is part of love and love evolves. Even the stage of "acceptance" is not final – it continuously shifts and changes. You do not get over your loss or get through it – you can move through it, continuously pushing forward and allowing the days to move you along, but you can never get over your loss or be finished with it. There is no other side to grief, yet it feels like climbing a mountain. You will never put it behind you, no matter how many years it's been – grief will always be a part of you – lurking and hiding, waiting to reappear. Grief is just love with no place to go, so with you and within you, it will stay. Tuck it away when you can, when you learn how to compromise with grief and when you must, because, well, the pasta aisle at the grocery store isn't really the best place to let it out (even though it will most certainly make an appearance at some point in time) but let it out when it wants and needs to see the world. Don't try and hide from grief. Don't try and force yourself to be strong or appear in a fashion deemed necessary for the place and time; your grief is your own journey, and no one can lead you to take a certain path.

Grief is unique. The loss may be similar, the relationship may be the same, but grief is not. What one person can handle, may not be what you can handle. Don't apologize for what you can't handle. You don't have to abide by the rules set forth by the books and websites, groups, and professionals. Some may give advice on how they handled their grief, but that is how THEY handled THEIR grief. Grief is personal. Grief is possessive. Grief is not simple, not explainable, not understandable.

There are many sayings and clichés that you will hear as you experience grief; however, there are no words to magically make it better. Even though I have experienced grief for many years, I don't even know what to say to make it better. All I have are my own words that describe my grief - words that I have shared within these pages. Within these pages, you will see how grief has reared its ugly head and taken over my life. You will see how I feel about the stages, steps, and waves of grief! Through these pages, I put into words decades of love and passion, hopes and dreams, and the destruction of decades of what I should have had. Through these pages, I attempt to give grief a resting place. Although I know deep within, grief will never rest, I place it safely where it will not bellow – I place it into my widow's web.

Still

People coming by-
yet I'm Still Alone.
Phone calls, texts, messages-
but I Still have no one to talk to.
Cards, gifts, donations-
Still, I have nothing.

Paperwork and forms to fax,
emails to send,
decisions to make,
deadlines to meet,
a checklist with tasks complete-
yet there is Still so much to do.

Still.

"It will get easier with time," they say-
but time stands Still.
Nothing makes it better-
the pain will Still exist.
I will never feel joy again-
you are Still gone.

Still.

You are gone-
but they Still get to live.

Still.

Should. Instead.

I should have called.
I said I would.
I went to sleep instead.
"I'll talk to him in the morning," I said.
Morning never came.

They should have done more.
It was their job.
They let you die instead.
"We're so sorry," they said.
Everyone is sorry.

You Should be here.
I'm alone Instead.

Six.

I've got your six.
Check by. Back up. Assist.
Brother. Sister. Partner.

Lies.

Let Her Cry

Tears.
Fighting back all day.
Some get by.
Not the right time. Wait until later.
Leave the room. Go outside.

It hurts.
Pain.
Misery.
Unbearable.
Agony.
Never ending.

I think you will call. You might text me.
Maybe you're running late.
I think you will be home soon.
I forget. I remember.
Why do I forget. I wish I didn't have to remember.

It hurts.
Pain.
Misery.
Unbearable.
Agony.
Never ending.

Taking the kids places. Family outings.
Only five now. Incomplete family.
At the store. See something you like.
Songs that make me think of you.
A smile or laugh sneaks by. Guilt sets in.

It hurts.
Pain.
Misery.
Unbearable.
Agony.
Never ending.

Morning comes.
The night is over.
Maybe it was all a dream.
I wake up.
Every day again.
Stuck in this hellish day.
Nothing has changed.
Nothing is better.

It hurts.
Pain.
Misery.
Unbearable.
Agony.
Never ending.

They seem so strong. I am not.
They seem ok. I am not.
How can everyone move on.
How can they pretend.
How can they act like it's just another ole' day.
I feel hopeless. Helpless.
You are gone.
Forever.
Do they even care. Prayers, hopes, faith.

It hurts.
Pain.
Misery.
Unbearable.
Agony.
Never ending.

Smile. Stand tall.
Be strong.

Impossible.
Let her cry.

Something

I walk in the room,
looking for Something -
signs of life,
of return,
of your presence.
A supernatural occurrence,
a message,
Something.

I look at your phone,
scrolling for Something-
signs of life,
of return,
of your presence.
Photos and messages,
videos,
some I've never seen or have forgotten.
A recollection,
a reminder,
Something.

I sit in your closet,
hoping for Something-
signs of life,
of return,
of your presence,
Your clothes,
your uniforms,
your belongings,
items on the counter,
remnants in the sink,
laundry on the floor.

All is still. Waiting for you.
Waiting for Something-
signs of life,
of return,
of your presence.
Something.

But there is
Nothing.

A million times a day…
My thoughts-

I'll tell you when you wake up…
I'll tell you when you get home…
I'll text you and let you know…
I can't wait to show you…
I can't wait to see what you think…
I'll talk to you about it later…
Caleb will know…
Let me ask him…
You'll wake up in a little bit…
You'll be home soon…
You'll walk in the door any minute…
I think Caleb's home…
I think you're outside…
You'll take care if it later…
Caleb can do it…
Let me ask him…

A million times a day…
My tears.

Twenty

Twenty years is a lot.
In twenty years,
a tree has grown complete,
a boy becomes a man,
a girl becomes a lady,
a house can be paid off,
an education is fulfilled.

Twenty years is a lot.
You can do so much in twenty years.
You learn so much in twenty years.
You know so much in twenty years.
You should know what to do in twenty years.
You should know better after twenty years.
How can this even happen after twenty years.

Twenty years is a lot.
But your twenty has stolen my forever.

Excuses

It was dark.

> You have flashlights.

We didn't know.

> You could've said something.

We tried.

> You hesitated.

It was an accident.

> You were trained.

We're sorry.

> You get to go home.
> You get to continue.
> You get to move on.
> You get to do better.
> You get to forget.
> You get to try again.
> You get to live.

He doesn't.

God has turned his back on me,
but I can still see the guilt in his eyes.
There must be a sliver for the damage he has allowed.
Does he feel remorse for what he has done,
or does he simply shrug for the sake of free will is man's doing?
Does he feel the soul crushing pain I endure every second of the day,
or does he look away and search for new prey?
As I fall to my knees begging, crying out, screaming-
Does he even listen?
Does he even care?
Prayers are meaningless. Talking to the air.
God does not exist. What a waste of time.
Miracles are simply luck.
And that I have none.
I am a cursed heap of hopelessness.
Nothing can repair.
Overcome with breathless brokenness.
Unable to fathom the lonely days ahead.
Forced to be a part of this wretched life.
Alone.
Without my love.

But Now-

You all look normal to me.
Nothing strange or unsettling.
You have gentle smiles.
You might have all been friends.
Not much older. Not much younger.
Nothing out of the ordinary.
I look at your photos,
I read about your lives.
I even speak your names.
You look kind.
You look like one of the good guys...

But now -
I want to rob you of your smiles,
like you robbed me of my life.
In less than five minutes you destroyed my whole world.
You failed us.
You failed your oath.
How could you be so stupid.
You looked kind.
You looked like one of the good guys...

But now –

Every Second
Gasping,
Choking,
Crushing,
Pain rushes thru -
Taking over my existence.
Cement fills my chest.
My breath is ripped from my lungs as tears flood my eyes.
My heart aches -
Burning,
Swelling,
Throbbing.
Flames rage my soul.
My strength is diminished -
I can't move.
Paralyzed with sorrow.
Grief fills my veins.
I am lifeless,
Useless,
Hopeless.
Breathe.
Wipe your face.
Stand up...
...Repeat.

Stuck on Repeat

I'm in a holding pattern.
Stuck on repeat.
I can't break free.
I feel like I'm always waiting for something.
I feel like something will happen.
I don't know what.
Nothing will happen.
Nothing can happen.
You are gone.
I wake up and you are still gone.
But this feeling of waiting is still here.
Why do I wait?
Why do I feel this way?
I feel nothing but pain.
Endless.

Stuck on repeat.

Drowning

I am drowning in a sea of helplessness.
Anchored to the dark hatred depths of despair.
You are my lifeline and the only chance of survival,
but your rope I cannot reach.

Stretch.
    Give me your hand.
        Throw the rope once more.
            Come closer.
                I can't tread much longer.

With every wave of suffocating tears,
I float further and further away.
I can't see you.
I can't hear you,
Your presence is no longer here.
How can I find hope.
How can I find an end.
I gasp for air.
I long to breathe your gentle touch once more.
I reach out.
Hoping I'll find a way.
Hoping I'll forget the pains of these endless days.
Hoping to wake up.
Hoping to breathe again.
The air is thin.

Stretch.
    Give me your hand.
        Throw the rope once more.
            Come closer.
                I can't tread much longer.

I can't reach you.
I can't find you in the black caverns of emptiness.
I am alone.
I am without you.

Stretch.
    Give me your hand.
        Throw the rope once more.
            Come closer.
                I can't tread much longer.

I gasp.
No air.
I need your air.
Breathe for me.
Breathe again.
One of us has to breathe.
Find the air.
Breathe.
Find the air.
Keep it for yourself if you cannot share.
I'll let go if it means you get to live again.
Your heart has to beat.
Open your eyes.
Breathe.
Reach out to me.

Stretch.
    Give me your hand.
        Throw the rope once more.
            Come closer.
                I can't tread much longer.

                I can't tread much longer.
                    I can't tread much.
                        I can't tread.
                            I can't.
                                I.

Pick Up

I sit alone.
I call out.
I cry.
Longing for you to answer.
But you don't hear my calls.
Is anyone listening.
Pick up.

My tears are too heavy to bear.
Day after day.
How many more days must I hold on to these lonely breaths.
Pick up.

I'm calling.
They say you're there.
They say you can hear me.
Why won't you pick up.
They say you are watching.
Looking down.
By my side.
I'm calling.
Pick up.

Someone pick up.
It's me.
Can you hear me.
Pick up.

- - - - - - - - - -

I'm Sorry

It's too quiet.
Where is your loud, booming voice I used to complain about.
I won't complain anymore.
Talk.
Don't worry about the volume.
Speak to me.
Talk for hours.
We all want to listen.
> I'm sorry I tried to quiet you.

Laugh.
Loud goofy, embarrassing.
I want to bottle it up and keep it for a rainy day when my tears flood the earth.
Watch what you want to watch.
I'll let you pick.
I won't change the channel or get annoyed.
Play your music.
I won't poke fun. I won't turn up the tv.
> I'm sorry I tried to quiet you.

Touch my hand. Pull me close.
I won't shy away.
You think I'm beautiful.
I believe you now.
I won't push you away.
I want you to hold me.
Tender kisses that could last for hours.
> I'm sorry I tried to quiet you.

Call me.
I will answer.
I will listen.
Tell me everything.
Or just sit in silence knowing we are both there like we did when we were young.
Send me a message.
I will reply.
I'm not too busy.
You are my everything.
I've turned off the world.
I am here.
Waiting.
> I'm sorry.

Without You

Aching,
Gasping,
Heaviness.

Pounding,
Crushing,
Emptiness.

Dark,
Blinding,
Loneliness.

Crippled

I am crippled.
Crippled by the unknown-
Not knowing what really happened,
What was said or not said,
What was done or not done.
They say I can't know yet.
They say it will be too hard.
They say give it some time.
They say it takes time.
They say get some help.
Nothing will help.

I am crippled.
Crippled by the whys-
Why did this happen?
Why didn't he do what he was supposed to do,
what he was trained to do,
what he should have known to do?
Why didn't the radios work?
Why didn't he just speak out?
Why did they even take the call?
Why don't they have better equipment?
Why didn't the vest cover more?
Why couldn't the shot have been 1 inch to the left?
Why did it take so long to communicate, to dispatch, to get help?
Why couldn't they have gotten there sooner?
Why won't they tell me anything?
Why?

I am crippled.
Crippled by the tears-
The flooding tons of burning, ice covered cries that consume my existence.
Crippled by the rusted, jagged, blades of regrets that shred my thoughts and rip my breath away.
Crippled by the piercing, sawing knives of pain that scar my insides and leave me lifeless.
Crippled by the all-consuming awareness of knowing I have to get up every day and live it all again.
Crippled by this continuous, infinite loop of no end.

No end to the unknown.
No end to the whys.
No end to the tears.
No end to the regrets.
No end to the pain.
No end to the awareness.
No end to this crippled life I am left to bear.

I am crippled.

Friday

Every Friday feels like that Friday.
I can't shake the feelings away.
I live them all over again every week, as if it is live in real time.
The day feels long, and time stands still.
I look at the clock and it seems to be stuck, paused, frozen.
The day never seems to really end, and it's like it's on repeat anyways-
so it never actually ends.
Every Friday I think it's a do over, a new start.
Maybe I'll wake up and the nightmare will be over.
It was a horrible prank, a misunderstanding.
But every Friday it's still the same.
I reach for my phone, check the time, look out the window.
It feels like you could still come home.
It kills me every time I think it.
You will never come home again.
I will never hear your voice, see your face, feel your touch.
Never again will I feel joy, feel peace, feel love, feel ecstasy.
Never again.
It will always be Friday.

Mornings

Mornings are the hardest-
I should roll over and see your face.
I should snuggle up against you;
it was always my safe place.
I should reach out through the blankets and feel your soft, strong arms;
grasp our hands together- always knowing there I faced no harm.
I should hear your gentle breathing, often with a funny snore.
Sometimes getting louder, unable to ignore.
I'd give you a bit of a nudge-
you'd breathe in, open your eyes a little, and budge-
softly whisper, "sorry."
It's the way it always was.
I'd put our heads together, smile, and kiss your head;

I didn't want to wake you, you had just gone to bed-
but I longed to hear the stories of your night,
find out how you'd been.
You'd always say the same thing, "it was fine."
Always wanting to guard me from the sin.
You knew I didn't like to hear of the dangers of the job,
or the sadness and pain you had to face,
the joy people tried to rob.
I would let you sleep more,
so you could gain your strength.
If you slept past a certain time,
back to the bed I would creep -
hoping you would open your eyes, stretch, and face the day.
The late afternoon and evenings,
by your side is where I'd stay.
Running errands, getting work and tasks complete.
Rarely did we have nothing to do-
always busy through the week.
We would try to find a few moments to just sit and be-
those moments were few and far in between,
but I will treasure those memories.
Every morning I wake again,
and you are no longer there-
gone is my warmth and happiness-
the bed seems so bare.
I imagine you sleeping,
and play back in my mind-
open my eyes again and again,
hoping that just one time-
one time you'll return,
and this pain will come to an end-
my love will be home and
my mornings will be beautiful again.

Anger

Anger fills my soul -
breeding flames that rip through my body like a disease, filling every cavity with vengeance.
Why does a God so gracious and full of love let something so tragic happen?
Why does a God who I believed in turn away and let me suffer?
Why does man have so much power to be able to take one's life?
Why didn't he look or speak out or take just a moment to think?
If the house was clear, why did he have his gun at all?
Why couldn't you have been somewhere else at that time or just taken a break and not worried with it?
Why weren't you the first to enter or the one who offered to stay outside?
They say it was an accident, but "I'm sorry" won't fix this.
They say the radios didn't work-
had y'all been able to speak to each other you would still be here!
I'm angry at the ones who choose to make excuses!
I'm angry at the ones who won't fix the problems!
I'm angry at the one who didn't do his job!
I'm angry at the ones who didn't protect you like they said they would!
I'm angry that you went there at all!
I'm angry that I went to bed and didn't call you!
I'm angry at everyone who says it's God's plan!
I'm angry at all the prayers - useless talking to air!
I'm angry that I have to do everything alone!
I'm angry that the kids don't get to have you in their lives anymore!
I'm angry that you don't get to see them grow up!
I'm angry that our daughters will not have you walk them down the aisle!
I'm angry that our son has to learn how to be a man on his own!
I'm angry that our future grandchildren will never know you!
I'm angry that I didn't appreciate every second!
I'm angry that I didn't take in all your love every chance that I could!
I'm angry!
I'm angry!
I am angry that I'm angry and that I let the anger take control-
control my mind, control my will, control my drive!
I'm angry I have no answers and that I can't fix anything!
I'm angry that you're not here with me!
I'm angry that they gave him a job when he wasn't prepared for the task!
I'm angry that this stupid life has a stupid expiration date and that we spend years fully engulfed in love just for it to
be ripped apart and our joy to be replaced with anger!
It's a waste of time, a waste of breath, a waste of emotion.
Anger is a waste.
But anger is possessive and wrecks all in its path.
Anger is destruction,
anger is a release,
anger is normal they say,
anger will eventually go away they say.
How can this feeling go away when it's all I live and breathe?
When I'm not angry I'm suffering in grief.
I'd rather be angry and scream than be consumed with breathless suffering.
Anger fuels my soul.

Our Last Night

If I had known it was our last night,
I would've held on a little longer.
I would've closed off everything around,
so we could just lay there and hold each other.
One more kiss and then one more and one more for good measure -
stayed right there in your arms and ignored the world forever.
I would have captured every moment, remembered every word,
done everything to stop the time,
anything that I could.
I would have lassoed the sun and put it in a box,
sealed it with a lock so tight,
the next day would be forever lost.
The night would just go on and on, throughout all of eternity;
we could have stayed there together,
in infinite ecstasy.

A Broken Heart

There's a line in a song that says, "...can you die from a broken heart..."
Well, I think absolutely you can.
Maybe not right away and maybe not actually physically, but you die a little bit each day.

It starts with your brain-
You forget things, you can't remember what you were about to do or what you have scheduled for the day. You can't focus, you're easily distracted. You find yourself driving down the road and then suddenly realize that you've gone so many miles and don't recall traveling that far or suddenly you realize that you've slowed down and almost to a complete stop in the middle of the road because your mind has just shut down. You start forgetting things that were important to you, desperately digging into the back of your memories hoping to recall details and ending up frustrated and devastated that you can't remember something. You can't find things, so you destroy the house, looking everywhere only to end up empty-handed.

After your mind has died it moves on to what little emotion you have left.
Your joy dies with each second of the day- finding something to be happy or thankful for in the day is impossible. The few brief moments where you do find yourself smiling or laughing over something just fills you with an incomprehensible and overwhelming wretchedness of regret and guilt, so you keep yourself from doing anything that might risk bringing any joy.

You would think that a broken heart would cause you to be possessed with fears, but it's just the opposite. Slowly all your sense of reality and reasonable comprehension begins to die. You don't care about the risks that anything brings; you no longer think logically. Who cares if there is danger-death means an end to the gut-wrenching pains of the broken heart.

Your motivation slowly dies next.
Each day it gets harder and harder to want to exist or complete any task. Even things that are important and necessary and helpful seem useless and mundane. Your purpose in life is gone so why bother with anything anymore.

Once your brain is dead, your emotions and rationality have passed on, and your motivation cease to exist, you are left with just a shell of rotting flesh that seems to carry you through each day like a robot, on auto pilot, just following the routine of the days but with no sense of existence.

Yes, absolutely you can die from a broken heart.

If you are not physically dead soon, you wish sometimes you were. Anything to stop the pain, end the suffering, heal the broken heart.

Nothing mends a broken heart.

Okay.
Good.
Alright.
Fine.

That's what people want to hear.
That's what you're supposed to say.

It doesn't matter what I say.
They're all just lies.

The Friends of Grief

If you thought anger was a disease or envy a plague,
unforgiveness a war zone or jealousy a blaze,
then you've never known the monster, regret.

Regret is the real demon, the devil of sorts,
the evil spirit that comes in and destroys while you work.
Regret starts by putting your stomach in knots,
slashing your heart until it can't beat,
ripping your spirit,
and putting your hopes and joy to sleep.
It makes you go mad and wish it would all end,
begging for a second chance -
anything to make yourself sane again.
You would do anything to feel a bit of peace,
make a deal with the devil,
steal, stomp, crush - anything for ease.
The "what ifs" and "should haves" are evil twins that laugh at the sight of your tears;
they mock your cries and fill your thoughts with fears.
You wish for a do-over, a mulligan, another try-
begging, screaming, pleading-
but regret smirks at the cry.

If you don't feel regret,
your soul is full of guilt,
and you've never experienced pain
until you meet the wickedness of -
secrets.

That is where you truly feel killed.

Belongings

His clothes are still on the floor,
his counter remains untouched.
The empty bottle on the table -
trash - but it means so much.
I have his wallet, keys, and phone-
holding them close gives me a false sense that I'm not really alone.
To see all his things fills my heart with grief;
I should put everything away and maybe gain some relief.
But the thought of moving forward consumes me with guilt,
I can't touch a thing, or I risk damaging the life that we built.
What if he comes home and wonders where things are?
The thought makes me sound crazy-
a fact I can't ignore.
I know he is gone, with no chance of return,
but I still can't move a thing -
the hope of reuniting is all that I yearn.
One day, maybe...months or years from now,
I'll find the strength, somehow.
Into a box, a bin of sorts, into the closet they will go,
but his memory, his love, and all that we had,
will never leave my soul.

Wishes

I wish you knew how many people came to pay their respects.

I wish you knew how beautiful the ceremony and everything was.

I wish you knew how many people have come by, called, and helped.

I wish you knew how many cards and gifts were sent.

I wish you knew from all over the country the love and support that's been shown.

I wish you knew all the great things that people have said about you.

I wish you knew how much it hurts and how much we miss you.

I wish you knew how hard I'm working to keep everything together.

I wish you knew that I've been cooking dinner, keeping up with the laundry, and keeping the house clean every day.

I wish you knew I was waking up early to take care of all the animals.

I wish you could see how beautiful your flower garden and pond has stayed.

I wish we could spend our evenings pulling weeds together.

I wish you knew how great the kids were doing and how I wish I had their strength.

I wish you could be here to help Mark get ready for the year.

I wish you were here the day he needs to shave.

I wish you were here when he brings home a girl he plans to wed.

I wish you could tell him how to be an amazing husband like you were.

I wish you were here to see how great at baking Lizzie is getting.

I wish you were here to work out with Annie and get her ready for Boot Camp.

I wish you were here to send your silly memes to Rosalan and to connect with her like I can't.

I wish you were here to help me get through each day.

I wish you were here to watch our babies grow up.

I wish you were here to see them dance and cheer and play.

I wish you were here for graduations and on their wedding day.

I wish you could be here in a few years when we become grandparents, too young to be, even in a few years, but that day will surely come.

I wish they could meet their Pops.

I wish we could retire and open our business in the mountains like we've always dreamed about.

I wish I could grow old with you like we've planned for many years.

I wish I could hold you and feel your touch once more.

I wish I could kiss you and hold your hand and look into those beautiful eyes.

I wish I could hear your voice and hear your laugh as loud and annoying as it is.

I wish you were here to watch your stupid shows and listen to your goofy music.

I wish I could have you help me with all the big pans.

I wish you were here to change the lightbulb in the pantry that I can't get fixed.

I wish you could figure out the timer on the dryer.

I wish we could sit in our his and hers rocking chairs.

I wish you knew I was staying strong just for our babies.

I wish you knew how much I want to just give up.

I wish you knew how much I love you and how much pain I'm in.

I wish you knew how much I need you and how I'm falling apart.

I wish I could tell you how much you mean to me.

I wish you knew how important you are and how I can't live without you.

I wish I could talk to you and see you and feel your arms around me.

I wish you knew how many lives you touched and how the world aches without you.

I wish I could tell you I'm sorry for what a pain I was - complaining, nagging, griping.

I wish I didn't shut down when I was upset and push you away.

I wish I had spent every day with you and never missed a chance to love you.

I wish I didn't get irritated so easily.

I wish I had always said yes to your love.

I wish I didn't have rehearsal that night and that I had called you.

I wish you knew the world is better and brighter with you in it.

I wish you knew how much I need you each and every day and how every moment without you is the worst pain I've ever felt.

I wish I had more wishes, and I could wish you back again.

Black Hole

Losing you has thrown me into a Black Hole.
A black hole of infinite Pain and Sorrow.
A void full of Nothingness.
It is Empty.
Dark.
Cold.
I am Lonely.
I am Numb.
My heart has stopped.
My soul ripped out.
My purpose for life removed.
My place in this world no longer exists.
I cannot breathe.
I function only out of necessity,
by no choice of my own.
You are gone.
I am gone.

Purpose

Loving you gave me a purpose for living.
At a time in my life when everything was a mess,
your love straightened my path and redirected my journey.
Your love made me feel limitless.
Your love gave me wisdom.
One touch of your hand gave me all the strength to face the demons
of this world, of my mind, and of my past.
Your love made me feel like I could move mountains.
Loving you made me beautiful, confident, and real.
Loving you let me know I had nothing to fear.
One kiss and I floated beyond the stars.
Loving you gave color to a gray world and brought life to a deaden limb.
Your eyes, your smile, your arms around me –
the recipe for unending joy and happiness.
Loving you gave me life.
Loving you gave me reason.
You were the reason for my life.
Without you, what reason do I have left to live...

You Are

You are in the sunset,
all the colors of the sky-
streaks of peace and beauty,
the daylight's sweet goodbye.

You are in the moon,
the luster of the night-
the glistening of the stars,
the wonder streaming bright.

You are in the sunrise,
as the morning says hello-
waking the world's creatures
with a warm but gentle glow.

You are in the flowers,
the wind within the trees-
the loving calls of nature,
the dewdrops on the leaves.

You are in the mountains,
the river's mighty stream-
you are in the hills and lakes,
the waves as the ocean's dream.

As the storms rumble throughout the land,
and the earth blares and shouts,
you are in the promise of better days,
as the rainbow's arc comes out.

As I wake, as I sleep, as my heart takes a beat,
you are in my every thought-
when I smile and I weep.

You are in my every move,
as I breathe and carry on-
you give me strength to meet the day
and to face the nights alone.

The thought of your smile and your laugh
makes my sorrows seem to fade;
never shall I have to fear-
for your love's so strong it will last for all my days.

Until we reunite again,
your memories I will hold,
they'll give me faith and hope,
so I can meet you on the streets of gold.

Your Hate Fuels My Gratitude

There are many who don't like the police right now-
the hate, the cruel words, the violence is abound.
I know some officers have been too tough;
some act cynical, a few abuse their power, and many often judge,
but if you ask them all why they chose the blue line,
they would all say to protect you and to deter crime.
To be there for you in your time of need -
they actually hate writing tickets when you run red lights or speed.
They don't condone the wrong that's been done,
and all shouldn't be punished for the acts of just some.
Behind that badge is a heart of strength,
that hides so many battles of fear and grief.
They mourn for the ones whose lives have been taken,
the crashed cars, the abused, the overdosed lost soul that will never be awakened.
You don't see them break down after these wretched calls.
You don't know they too want changes to fall.
They want justice, freedom, and the guilty to pay.
They support you, they care, just in a different way.
So before you want to curse them or if danger upon them is what you wish,
I beg of you to stop and imagine this:
The road backed up and lined for miles,
every parking lot surrounding the church is piled.
High from a ladder, an American flag waves,
and the line of saluting officers goes on for days.
Slow and steady steps with your head held high,
in your heart comes an overwhelming sense of gratitude and pride.
They stand there at attention bearing the heat,
holding back tears for you and your children they weep.
They didn't all know your husband that well (some not even at all),
but there they still stand-
some with heavy hearts who tried to respond to the call.
"Officer down," all the radios filled,
and through the streets, sirens and red and blue spilled.

There was nothing they could do, yet they all fled;
now here they stand as their lips quiver, and their eyes are all red.
They try to stay strong as the 21 shots fill the air,
as the bugle and pipes play the song that is too hard to bear.
They stand there and watch as the flag is folded tight,
as it's passed to the family, the tears they have to fight.
They try to ignore the wife's screams of pain,
and the worst sound of all is when dispatch calls his name.
He doesn't answer, they call a few times-
"14 Charles 12, 14 Charles 12...Come in...14 Charles 12"
They try once more and then the last call comes and they close out the line.
He is carried away and into the car he goes-
slowly their salute is released, and their arms drop back low.
They can wipe the sweat from their brow and let the tears flow down.
One last pass by the wife and the kids,
then back to the streets where the evil all lives.
Hoping for safety for a shift full of grace,
his brothers and sisters in blue return back to the race.
Back to protect you, to keep you all safe;
back to a world that is filled with all hate.
Back to the signs with messages so foul,
back to the dark streets where the enemy can prowl.
Stop and think what the world would be like
if the monsters were let loose and alone you had to fight.
The blue line is there so you can rest at ease;
they take on the storms so you can feel the breeze.
Give them a chance, walk in their shoes;
give them the respect that is profoundly due-
And pray you never have to follow behind the sea of blue,
as you head to the last place your husband will lay,
because that officer you hate -
will be crying with you that day.

You Are Still Gone

Woke up this morning -
you were still gone.
Maybe I thought today would be different;
maybe I thought everyone was wrong.
Each day moves by so slowly,
as if I am stuck in a time lapse.
I just want to see you, hear you, feel you.
I just want all of this pain to pass.
Your photos surround me so I can see you everywhere,
but it's not the same.
It's not really you.
All your things stay as they were -
a mausoleum of sorts - a tribute.
Your videos and messages I play on repeat;
I cry out and speak to you.
You don't reply. You don't answer.
You are gone. I know it is true.
I still beg for your return.
I still look for a message, a sign.
I can't shake the feeling that you will come back some time.
I know it sounds crazy.
I know you are gone.
I know I am alone and there is nothing I can do. I must just move along.
So, I am here to continue living -
when all I want to do is whither away to nothingness and be reunited again.
All I want is to feel your arms wrapped around me; my head tucked so perfectly beneath your chin.
Is there a Heaven? Are you there?
Will I see you again?
Have faith. Believe.
I must force myself to go along.
The hope is all I have to push me through as I wake each morning,
and you are still gone.

So Many Things

So many things to tell you
about life, the kids, and such.
So many things to show you -
you've missed out on so much.
So many things I wish I had said,
so many regrets I will never forgive.
I wish I could go back in time
to show you how much I valued that you were mine.
Each day I miss you more and more, and the pain becomes too much to endure.
I need you here, I need you home.
I'm so tired of being alone.
This isn't how our life was meant to be -
we had so many plans and dreams.
But now each day I am without you, and each day is full of suffering.
The kids need their father and I need my love.
I need your arms around me and the beauty in your eyes.
I need the calming sound of your voice.
Nothing else helps, believe me I've tried.
It's not fair. This wasn't the plan.
Nothing makes sense anymore.
Nothing will ever be good again.
I need you. It's all I long for.
So many tears I have cried
and so many sleepless nights.
If only there was a cure,
but nothing can make this right.

One more day without you
is one more day closer to seeing you again.

I wasn't raised a true Christian; we didn't go to church, we didn't read the Bible or pray, but I was told stories from the Bible, and we occasionally talked about Jesus and God and all that. My grandparents would invite me to church a few times through the years, but I didn't really know about faith and God's love until high school. I started to attend church with my grandparents a little more often during the summer between my junior and senior year of high school. I joined the girls' ministry and became very interested in learning more about salvation. I guess God was preparing me, because my mother died at the beginning of my senior year. I do believe it was my faith and newfound relationship with God that helped me not completely go off the deep end.

I still believe – or at least I try to, I want to. It is so hard to believe and trust in a deity that would allow so much pain and evil to roam. How could a loving god take my dad from me when I was only a little girl, my brother just a baby – take my mother from me in my essential years when a young lady needs her mother and take her in such a horrific way – take her husband, her best friend, her love, her companion, her partner, her soulmate, her everything, the father of four children who need a dad, who need their dad. How can I trust and have faith that He loves me and rejoice and praise His name? I just don't understand. Why does this person get spared, get a miracle, a cure, survive, get rescued…but this one ignored?

I don't know if there really is a Heaven and a Hell. I don't know if there is a God and Jesus. I don't know if my husband is up there with them, waiting for me…. but I'll tell you this much – I sure hope it's true. That hope is the only thing that keeps me going some days. The hope that a beautiful paradise awaits me and that I will see my mom and dad again. That my love is there and will pull me back into his arms once again. I sure hope so. I'd rather try and believe and be wrong (I won't even know if I am), than give up the last mustard seed of faith I have and find out it was all true and miss out. I have to keep the faith; I have to believe; I have to hope.

"Remember, hope is a good thing, maybe the best of things, and no good thing ever dies."
-Stephen King

John 16:22

Caleb

I cried myself to sleep last night,
but that is nothing new-
I cry myself awake each day,
and until the day is through.

Sometimes my tears are empty,
but the cries still seem to flow.
I can't catch my breath, my body drops,
and I then I lose control.

The loneliness is unbearable,
and the regrets are taking their toll-
I am drowning in this wicked pain,
and the grief is wrecking my soul.

Why does this misery get to win,
and win again each day?
Why do I have to face this world,
and pretend like I'm okay?

I'm not okay, nothing's fine,
and no, it won't ever be.
Time does not heal all wounds,
and God must be ignoring me.
Don't waste your breaths on senseless prayer-
trust me, they don't help.

I just have to face the day without him,
and endure the suffering I've been dealt.
If only time would reverse and the sequence
of events could change;
if only people would have done things right,
he would still be here, and my joy would remain.

He didn't deserve this act of betrayal -
he did nothing wrong-
he was a good man with love and heart,
and brought a sense of life wherever he was along.

He was there to help and do his job,
it brought him joy and pride,
but the careless acts of man and men
have robbed him of his life.

He had so much to give to all,
and everyone would agree,
that when Caleb was by your side,
you could laugh and smile so easily.

His energy and rush for life
was unique and made me you smile;
he had a way with words and stories,
that made things worth the while.

If ever you needed to know anything,
Caleb would knew what to say,
and if ever you needed a laugh or joke,
he was there to save the day.

His loud voice, his silly laugh,
his sweet, crooked grin,
his eyes like the sea and gentle spirit
that would just rope you in.

You knew you were good, and he had your back,
if ever he was near,
and the world was just such a better place,
whenever he was here.

But from now on all we have are our memories,
and all we can do is think of him and cry,
as we feel his love in the day's cruel breeze.

He is gone and his laugh is no more,
but I have to just keep pushing thru-
and hope someday, with all my soul,
that I'll be welcomed into eternity by my sweet,
Caleb Daniel Rule.

Had. But Now.

I've Had a police vehicle at my house almost daily for nearly 15 years.
But Now my driveway is empty.

I've Had a duty belt and gear in the top drawer for nearly 15 years.
But Now the dresser sits empty.

I've Had a gun locked away every day for nearly 15 years.
But Now the safe is empty.

I've Had stories with people mentioned by last name or badge number only for nearly 15 years.
But Now there's no one mentioned at all anymore.

We've Had a weekly schedule of extra jobs and classes for nearly 15 years.
But Now the calendar is bare.

I've Had his hand to hold, his eyes to capture my heart, and his voice to give me comfort for nearly 20 years.
But Now my world has nothing.

Walls

These walls are covered in your photos.
Photos of your life.
Photos of our love.

These walls are full of stories, trips, and memories.
The years of joy, happiness, and life's moments.

These walls have your presence.
The everlasting blessing of your existence.

These walls are a reminder of the precious gift you were to us all.
The energy you brought to a room.
The laughter you created.
The sounds of your booming voice, full of endless knowledge and information.

Full of humor.
Full of experiences that provided security and confidence.
Full of comfort.

These walls contain all that I have left to remember and honor you.

As I look around, these walls guide me through thousands of smiles, thousands of memories,
and now the thousands of tears that fill the room, flowing and flooding through these walls.

Breathe

The air thins.
Darkens.
Blurs with pain.
I'm choking.
Gasping.

Clenching for air.

Breathless.

Lifeless.

My body caves.
My soul quakes.
My heart is broken.

I'm drowning.
Drenched in tears.
Fight or flight.
Breathe or die.

Give in.
Give up.

No cure.
No remedy.
Nothing helps.
No aide.

Call for help.
Cry for help.
Nothing.
No one.
Alone.
Help.

Breathe.
Gasp.
Choke.

Cement pours over me.
The walls collapse.
Time stands still.
Yet the world moves on.
Keeps going.
Everyone pushes forward.
Everyone else breathes.
Blinks.
Hearts beat.
Footsteps.
Thoughts.
Memories.
Smile.
Laugh.
Shed a tear.
Wipe it away.
Breathe.
Everyone.
Me.

Choking.

Gasping.

Endless.

Eternal.

Black hole.
Breathe.

Not Ok

Not a cry for help. Just Facts.
I am not OK.
Quit asking me how I am doing.
It is a stupid question.
How do you think I am doing.
How should I be doing.
What is the right answer to that question.
Do you really want me to answer that question honestly or are you looking for a candid answer.
No, I am not doing well.
I am not stronger than I think.
Don't tell me I look good.
Don't tell me I am in your thoughts or that you are praying for me.
I prayed for my husband's safety every day for nearly 20 years and look with that got me.
What exactly are you praying for anyways.
You're praying for comfort for me.
How am I supposed to get comfort when I am alone without the love of my life.
He was my comfort.
God is not my comfort.
Don't tell me to lean on him.
He let my husband be taken from me.
Where was his comfort at 2 AM.
Where was his strength at 2 AM.
Where was he.
Can you answer that question.
No.
Then don't tell me that God is here for me.
Everyone said they would be here if I needed them.
Everyone said just ask if you need anything.
Every time I ask, only a few respond.
Everyone said we would not be forgotten.
Everyone said they would stick around, wouldn't go anywhere.
Only a few call to check on me.
Only just a few come by.
Everyone gets busy.
Everyone has their own life.
Everyone has their priorities and things they have to do for their own families.
I understand.
It is what it is.

Everyone else will move on.
Everyone else will move forward.
Many will probably even forget.
Some it will be days, maybe even weeks months, years before he pops into their mind again.
Only just a few times will they have a memory, a thought, have to wipe away tears.
I am drowning in my tears.
I am flooded with memories.
Every second of every second of every second, of every moment of every moment, of every minute of every minute, of every hour, of every day and day and day.
I don't get to just wipe away my tears and move on and move forward.
The only thing that gets me going each day is the fact that I must.
I don't have a choice.
I have four children that I must continue for.
If I didn't have to keep going and put one foot in front of the other for them, I wouldn't.
I would rather just lay in bed all day.
I would rather just stay in the closet and hold his clothes all day.
I don't want to do anything but be with him in some way in some form. But I don't have a choice.
That was taken from me when he was taken from me.
When the county decided not to hire and train properly.
When that sorry excuse for a man and officer decided to not use his training from over twenty years and take ONE DAMN SECOND TO LOOK at what the sound was.
I don't get to be strong.
I have to.
So don't tell me that I'm doing well.
I am not.
I don't have the choice to do well or not.
If you really want to help, send me a message, call me, come by the house. I can't ask for help because I need help with every single thing, and no one can do that.
No one can do what I actually need help with.
No one can fix it.
No one can make it better.
There's nothing anyone can do.
I am not ok.

43

Things People Say

Everyone keeps saying,
"Is there anything you need...
If you need anything, just ask...
Whatever you need..."

I am so overwhelmed with grief,
I can't always think if I need anything.

Everyone keeps saying,
"You are in our thoughts...
We haven't forgotten you...
You are not alone...
Yet no one comes by.

Where are you.
Where is the help.

Can you even help.
Can you fix this emptiness.

No. You can't.

But thanks for offering.

One of the Steps

I picked up your clothes from the floor today,
I washed them and put them away.
Now the room seems so empty,
like I've just erased you all away.
I know I need to pick up your things and donate or pack and store,
and throw away the empty bottle,
the old receipts, and more,
but I just can't seem to find the strength -
when I try, it cuts me to the core.
If I leave everything where it is and was,
it's almost as if you are still here.
If I get rid of it all then I get rid of your presence as well,
at least that is what I fear.
What am I supposed to do and when?
Everyone says I will know the answer in time,
when it feels right, when I am ready-
but the pain is too real, and the pain is all mine.
No one else has to make these decisions;
no one else has to feel this way.
Everyone else gets to move on and look forward to easier and better days.
But here I am with no end in sight,
alone all day and alone all night.
Looking at your table, your counter, your chair-
knowing that as long as it sits as it is,
it's a constant reminder that you will never any longer be there.
But I have to leave it all as it is,
I need to leave everything be.
Your clothes are in the drawers,
but I just can't bear to move any more.
Maybe one day it will feel right,
maybe I will move some more things,
but today, tonight, and for right now,
I can't handle the pain that it all brings.

Surrender

Do you get pleasure from my pain?
Are you ignoring me when I cry out your name?
Am I just a pawn in your horrible torturous game?
You keep destroying my life again and again!

You ask us to believe, to trust, and have faith,
but then you put us through hell and laugh in our face.
I'm so sick of the tragedy that goes on in this place!
Is there a finish line to this miserable and horrid rat race?

Disease, murder, death, pain, and constant fear.
Haven't we all been through enough this year?
I have put up with this trauma my entire life!
I've had endless darkness and strife!

Why is it that I cannot forever sustain any joy?
Why do you treat my life like a worthless old toy?

Just leave me alone - I don't want to play this game anymore.
You've taken enough from me - I can't stand it much more.

Caleb was my everything, my true love, and best friend.
Why did you have to take him from us and make our happiness end?
Was there not some other way to test our strength?
I cannot be strong anymore with all this grief.
I can't withstand the loneliness and tears.
I cannot do this for years and years.
I just want my husband and this pain to end,
but there is no fix, remedy, or way to mend.
I must keep going and learn to live with the sorrow,
until my final day comes and there is no tomorrow.
I can only hope that I've done what I should,
and lived the right way with nothing but good.

I can only hope that there is an afterlife,
with a Heaven that gives us the chance to reunite,
and there waiting for me will be my love-
standing there with his arms open wide for me to run.
To hold onto him so tightly again,
is the wish and hope that I will have until the end.
So, until that beautiful and glorious day is here,
I will keep pushing though and hope it is near.
I hope that I've finished God's test.
I hope that He's seen I've done my best.
I can't take losing anyone else that I love.
I surrender to God, to the Lord up above.

John 16:22

Overwhelmed with Emotion

I look at your pictures, and I am overwhelmed with emotion.
I smile for the sight of you brings me comfort and joy,
but my eyes fill with tears for the sight of you brings me pain and sorrow as I shall never see your beautiful eyes looking back at me again.

I listen to your messages and watch your videos, and I am overwhelmed with emotion.
I am comforted for the sound of your voice makes me feel like you are still here,
but the sound of your voice takes my breath away with pain as I know the sound is only temporary and not in real time.

I hold your clothes near and look through your things, and I am filled with emotion.
I am content for a moment as all your belongings hold a piece of you, and as I hold them in my hand I can feel your touch,
but I also feel emptiness as they are all void of your scent and fingerprints forevermore.

I smile as our children laugh, and I am overwhelmed with emotion.
I feel a sense of peace for their light shines from within and I know it is from you,
but my heart aches as your light is but a memory and will only shine on through stories, thoughts, and your legacy.

As I hold our children near to me,
I hear your heartbeat,
I feel your gentle breath,
and I sense your presence.
I want so badly to never let go,
as they are the only thing I have left that is wholly you,
and you I cannot let go of but cannot ever hold again.

The Monster

Another day without you,
another night alone,
another day of facing this world all on my own.

We should have had our ever after
and not a "that's it, the end;"
instead I am left with this emptiness from losing my best friend.

My entire world was swept away,
taken from me, ripped, and thieved,
and now all that remains is a shell filled with pain you could never imagine, nor believe.

A loneliness and void follows me everywhere,
right at my side, beneath me,
like a shadow from the pits of despair.
It won't leave my side,
even when there is no light -
it is attached to me like a growth, dug in to my bones with claws and a deadly bite.
I can never shake it off,
for time can't heal this pain,
this monster of death will forever be within me and will eternally remain.

If Only

Each night I think about what our life was and should have been,
and each day I wake to this hole in my heart and to tears that will never end.
I can't go back in time, I can't erase that day,
I can't reverse the clock to 1:59 or tell you to stay away.

Instead, I live it again and again,
the words, the sights, the fear,
if only there was a way to have you back, I would forever hold you near.
I would savor every moment and I would never let you go,
I would love you with all my strength and might,
love and adornment would be all you would ever know.

If only I had one more chance, a do-over to try again,
I could be happy once more and my broken heart could finally find a mend.

Are You There, God? It's Me, Eden.

Why are some spared, some healed, some given a second chance while others are left to suffer, parish, die?

Why are some sent a guardian, an angel, a miracle, while others gasp for air and breathe their last breath?

Why do some get rushed to surgery and medical aide succeeds, while others are pronounced on the scene or on arrival, and never get to fight?

Who gets to choose which life means more than the others?

Why take one over another?

Why skip over those who deserve to suffer and take the one who meant so much to everyone he met, who had so much love to give, so much light and purpose - a father, a husband, a friend.

Why cut his life short and destroy his family but allow the others safety and a future?

God has a purpose.
God is in control.
God is with you.
God loves you.
Call out to Him.

Well, God -

Why weren't you there?
Why weren't you present?
Why did you look away at 2:00am?
Why not stop this horrific tragedy?
Did we not pray enough?
Did we not serve your kingdom in the ways you preferred?
Did we not believe with enough strength and faith?
Was this supposed to be a wake up call?
Was this supposed to make me reach out to you?
What did you intend to gain from this evil and torturous act?
What is the purpose behind this pain?

Why him?
Why us?
Why?

No excuse is good enough to make this destruction make sense!
No answer will ever ease our suffering!
Nothing will ever make this better!
Nothing!
Why?!
Nothing! No answer! No reply!
God?
Nothing.

No End

There is no end to the questions of what if and why.
There is no end to the would, could, and should haves and wasted time.
There is no end to the regrets, guilt, and shame.
There is no end to the suffering, sorrow, and pain.
There is no end to needing you, wanting you, and wishing you were home.
There is no end to feeling empty, lost, and alone.
There is no end to missing you and longing for your touch.
There is no end to searching for your presence-it's pointless, but I just miss you so much.
And even more than all of this, one thing is forever true -
there is no end to my infinite and eternal love for you.

They Call This Denial

Why can't I shake the feeling that you are coming home.
Is it just because I want it so badly that my mind holds on desperately.
I keep thinking you are at work or out of town for some reason.
I keep telling myself I will tell you something when you get home.
Your pictures seem so real. Your videos like you are right there for me to grab and hold on to.
I feel like you will call or walk through the door any minute.
I listen to your voicemails, and it feels like you are right here, and your voice is present.
I feel like you are minutes away from coming home.
I sit. I wait. I look out the window. I check the room, to see if you are here.
I know you are gone and never coming back but I can't shake the feeling.
I wish it would just go away because it hurts so much, but if the feeling goes away, it's like you really are gone.
It doesn't feel real.
I want to wake up from the horrible nightmare.
I want the day to end. This endless and repetitive day that goes on and on and on. Over and over and over again.
You'll be home in the morning.
You'll wake up this afternoon.
It's your day off, I'll get to sleep beside you tonight.
You'll call at lunchtime.
You'll text when you wake up.
Every day, I still check the schedule to wonder when you'll be home or awake so we can be together.
It's Monday, you'll wake up this evening.
It's Tuesday, you'll only sleep a little while and be up the rest of the day.
It's Wednesday, you will be home all day unless you have STEP, then you'll be home around 4:30 or 5:00.
It's Thursday, you'll be home for a little while this evening in between shifts.
It's Friday, you'll only be awake a little bit this evening.
It's Saturday, I'll let you sleep until about 4:00.
It's Sunday, you can sleep until about 3:00 or 4:00.
Our week is ruined. Gone. Over.
You are gone.
When will this pain be over.
You're never coming home again,
So, the answer is-
Never.

But. Yet.

I cry out, but no one hears.

I scream in agony, but no one hears.

I call for you.

I lay here alone.

My tears flood the pillow.

My face, red.

Eyes burn.

Why do I cry out if I no one will hear.

Why do I scream if no one hears.

Why do I call for you.

You can't hear me.

I have no more tears, yet they still flow.

I have no more strength, yet I still have to move.

I have nothing more to give.

You are my EVERYTHING.

You are gone.

You don't hear me cry, yet I still cry.

They Say

They say it is a blessing.
I call it blood money.

They say there is a purpose.
I say it is asinine.

They say it gets easier.
I say it is too hard.

They say he would want you to be happy.
I say my happiness is in him.

They say God has a plan.
I say this plan is pretty Fucked up!

Lasagna and a Balloon

Your voice is a comfort.
Even when I was mad at you, I longed for your call.
Even just a text.
Hoping you would reach out, get me out of my funk and force me to speak.
I listen to the three voicemails I have and I wish I could hear your voice again.
In real time.
Calling.
Now.
Sending me a text.
Our special texts we would often send.
"Lasagna" and "Balloon"
Random sweet messages.
Our secret stories.
I wish I had kept them all.
I wish you were here to talk to.
To hear your endless stories.
Your useless knowledge.
Your loud voice.
Your annoying laugh.
Right here.
Beside me.
The comfort of your voice that I need in all of this pain.
Your touch is intoxicating.
Even when I didn't want affection, when I pushed you away or felt smothered, I longed for you to reach out and grab me.
Just hold my hand.
Hug me.
Come up behind me when I was looking in the mirror, wrap your arms around me and pull me in close.
Smile that sweet, crooked grin.
I would push you away - not in the mood for your shenanigans.
You would try and lay close in the early mornings or late hours of the night.
I would shake you off - tired, asleep.
Now I hold the pillow, the teddy bear.
I feel ridiculous.
Like a child.
I want you here.
Right beside me.
The intoxication of your touch that gives me peace.
Your kiss is everything.

Those thin, delicate lips.
The sweet taste.
The chills and butterflies that I still felt just as I did that first kiss almost twenty years ago.
Taking my breath away.
Taking my body to a place of surrender.
Your kiss on the small of my back.
Your kiss on my neck.
Your kiss on my forehead.
Your kiss on my hand.
Your kiss on the top of my spine, that divot, the sweet spot that made me cave.
I long for those moments.
Few and far between.
The regret.
I should have kissed you every morning.
Every night.
Every day.
Your kiss is the only thing that gives me hope.
Your eyes take me to a place of ecstasy.
Oh, how I could gaze into those eyes and be swept away to a heavenly realm of nonexistence.
An escape from reality.
From fear.
From pain.
Ecstasy that is beyond any touch, any kiss, any moment of intimacy that only you can bring.
I need to see those eyes of love.
True and endless love.
I need to feel your love.
Right here.
Right beside me.
The ecstasy of complete freedom, safety, and adornment that only your eyes can bring.
Your voice.
Your touch.
Your kiss.
Your eyes.
Right here.
Right beside me.
I wish.
I want.
I long.
I need.

Who

Who will reach the top shelf for me,
Who will cook the meat that seems so gross to me,
Who will check my car when something is wrong,
Who will wipe down the counter behind the sink,
Who will pump my gas,
Who will make the bed in one swoop,
Who will make calls, pay bills, and handle important matters,
Who will fix things that break,
Who will pick up heavy things,
Who will complain when my strands of hair are everywhere,
Who will open jars,
Who will wash the big pans,
Who will take pictures,
Who will make Lizzie alfredo,
Who will buy the right cheese,
Who will take Annie shooting and tell her about cop stuff,
Who will fight over the temperature with me, go back and forth over the kitchen lights, and close the door when the dog opens it at night,
Who will send Rosalan food memes,
Who will play basketball with Mark and teach him to be a man,
Who will be there for him when he becomes a husband and a father,
Who will show him how to change the oil, change a tire, and do "man stuff",
Who will give permission when our girls bring home a gentleman and who will walk them down the aisle as that young man is filled with love,
Who will hold my hand as I walk thru life,
Who will kiss my neck as I fix my hair,
Who will smile at me from across the room and whisper "I love yous",
Who will fill my bed, fill my heart, fill my soul,
Who will I grow old with?
I can't do all these things alone.....
and the things I can do,
I just don't want to do alone.

Why Him?

Murderers, robbers, abusers,
predators, pedophiles, thieves-
evil, hateful, cruel, and vicious,
dishonest, dangerous, and wicked-
walking around, committing crimes, living happily - a waste of lives.
Drug dealers, gangsters, and criminals of all sorts,
people who hurt children - disgusting, the worst.
On our streets and in our towns,
next-door neighbors - they are all around.

But Caleb had to die...

A man of knowledge, with a love for life,
four beautiful children and a
devoted wife-
a man of God with trusting faith,
a servant's heart, a friendly face.
A friend to all, full of energy and light,
full of jokes and a heart of might.
Positive, loving, genuine, and kind,
a gift to this world -
he shouldn't have had to die.

God got it wrong; he made a mistake.
He drew the wrong name and now it's too late.
There's no going back or making it right;
It just isn't fair -
Caleb shouldn't have died.

So many others with no life to live;
he could have taken anyone else -
someone with no love to give.
He could have made the world a little better by taking the wrong;
instead, he did the unthinkable, and now without Caleb, we must march along -
lonely, full of pain, and wondering why...

Why, oh why, did Caleb have to die.

Puzzle Pieces

You were my everything and more.
You knew every part of my body, inside and out.
I never had to say slow down, speed up, right there, or stop.
I never had to adjust, guide you, or give you directions.
I never had to ask for more or tell you what I wanted.
I would always say that we were created exactly for each other -
that our bodies fit perfectly in tune,
like a puzzle,
a lock and key.
You knew the exact combination,
the right rhythm,
the beat.
If I ever began to feel I needed to ask for something,
you would suddenly respond in the moment right before -
as if you read my mind,
my body,
my soul.
I joked that you had gotten a manual somewhere - how could you know.
We were meant for each other,
made for each other,
written in the stars.

Waiting.
Hoping.

I lay here in the dark,
and the world seems to stand still.
Time does not pass,
or it just goes by so slowly I don't even realize.
I lay alone.

Waiting.
Hoping.

Perhaps this will be the last time.
Perhaps the night will stop.

The room is silent.
I lay here alone,
yet I stay on my side of the bed
as if you will be home in the morning.
The pillows sit upright, the blanket turned down,
space left just for you.
The light from the stars glimmer through the window;
the night begins.
I lay here.

Waiting.

Hoping.

The porch light is left on for you so you can see as you
walk through the late hours of the night...
(even though you always had a flashlight and didn't
need me to leave it on - I still do)
The bedroom door is left open for you so you can
quietly come in without making a stir...
(even though your steps woke me just before the
alarm was set to ring - I still wake).

Waiting.

Hoping.

The house is in order - clean and tidy.
The day is over and everything is in its place...
The children sleep-
their gentle innocence rests and they dream.
(They dream as if there is anything worth dreaming of.)

The night pushes forward.
It comes and goes.
The moon begins to fade.
The night is over...
but the emptiness is not.
The loneliness stays
even though the darkness disappears
and the light takes over.
Even as the sun returns
and the morning makes its appearance,
the emptiness does not budge.
The loneliness of night does not wither.
It does not lose strength, weaken, or break.
I lay here still.

Waiting.
Hoping.

The day begins,
but the pain of night does not end.
Now I lay here,
still alone,
and the world moves on.
The hands of time turn with speeding force,
but I lay here still.

Waiting.
Hoping.

The pain of the day begins its course.
The never-ending, vicious cycle of my new existence.
I lay here.

Waiting.
Hoping.

I rise to face my enemy.
I stand here now.

Waiting.
Hoping.

Victim Impact Statement

I stare at the page.
The title mocks me.
The lines and spaces taunt me.

Victim. Impact. Statement.

How can one verbalize the depths of this misery?
How can one write with enough eloquence to describe the depths of this despair?
How can one find the right terminology to explain the depths of this anguish?

The page remains empty.
The words escape me.
The pen sits untouched.
There are no words.
The language does not exist.
The vocabulary not developed.
There is no scribe. No dictation.
There is no way to fill this page.
Nothing can ever be said that even comes close to worthy of expressing this misery.
Nothing can delineate this despair.
No way to make intelligible this anguish.
There will never be a way to
clarify, translate, or elucidate
this misery,
this despair,
this anguish.
No colloquy.
No locution.
No confabulation.

Nothing.

Nothing will ever portray or expound the impact of such misery, despair, and anguish.

So -

I shall continue to stare at the page.
The words will forever mock me.
The lines and spaces wield to infinitely taunt me.

I stare at the page.
The words mock me.
The lines and spaces taunt me.

Victim.

Impact.

Statement.

Double Edged Sword

I want this pain to end, but the day I stop crying I feel is the day you fade away.

I want to be with you so badly, but my biggest fear is death.

I want to have faith and believe you are waiting for me in Heaven, but how can a gracious God allow such pain and sorrow.

I want to believe you are watching over me, but the Bible says there is no sorrow in Heaven - how can you be in Heaven watching over me but feel no sorrow?

I want to be strong and keep things going for you and the kids, but I am so tired from the burden of grief.

I have to wake in the morning and face the day, but every day without you gets harder and harder.

I want to be a good mother for our children, but being a single parent is too hard sometimes.

I want to remember everything about you, but every thought makes me fall apart.

I feel like you are with me, but I think it's just what I wish.

I want to believe in signs and messages, but I would have known for sure if I had gotten one by now.

I want to feel joy in some of life's moments, but how can I feel joy through this misery.

I want to live life and do things with the kids, but it kills me to do things without you.

I want to feel loved, but the love of my life is gone.

I want to stop crying, but the pain is too much.

The Day.

I wake up,
I face the day.

I don't want to, but if I don't -
what will they say.

I get out of bed; I tend to the home -
the pets, the kids, the chores...

Same routine, every day.
Same mundane crap and nothing more.

Alone again to fight this war;
alone with the evils of this world.

The kids have needs and more than just I
can resolve and make better so I just lie -

"Moment by moment, we're pushing through,
doing the best we can and that's all we can do."

Annie's away and I worry for her,
so far away and so many lessons to learn.

Rosalan has it the worst is all that I fear,
and I don't know how to help, so I just stay aware.

Mark is alone, now the man of the home,
left to become a man and all on his own.

Lizzie, the smallest, Caleb's young girl;
she has his spirit and was his whole world.

What do we do without our light?
How can I be a good mother alone in this fight?
With my own battles, my own grief, and unbearable pain.

I want to give up - this beast is too much to tame.
But I push through the day and pretend I am fine.

I hope all day it will end,
this monster of mine -
this cruel and evil leaper, this leach they call grief;

But I am a single mother, a solo parent, a widow-
and there's no sign of relief.

This is now my title and a part of my name,
my identity and all I have left to claim.

Every morning and all day, this is now my new life -
I hate it, I want nothing to do with this strife.

Many try to help, they search for the right thing to say,
but they don't understand what it's like to have to feel
this way.

The fears, the worries, the pain and the sorrow;
nothing anyone can do to help,
so I just wait til tomorrow-
maybe that's when it will all go away;
maybe tomorrow will be a better day.

I get through the hours just the best that I can,
and at the end of the day, I lay alone with the weight of
this life in just my small hand.

The world moves forward and at the night's end-
I wake up to the same thing,
and have to live this life

all

over

again.

We All Grieve

They can't compare,
they aren't the same.
You don't really know what it's like.
You may have some stressors,
you may have some pains,
but you just have some thunderstorms and I'm in a constant hurricane.
Think before you complain of the things you can change,
and the issues you get to face.
Your small battle is not a war,
and you can finish your race.
To vent, to release, to let it all out
is all good and well,
but please look at the perspectives and remember I'm in Hell.
Little things are not a big deal so be appreciative of what you have,
and think before you tell me that you understand.
You can't imagine, even if you've been through it, too.
It's not the same - this horrible "journey" grief puts you through.

Gone

Gone.

Shattered.

Broken.

Collapsed.

Torn, ripped, and shred.

My heart, my soul, and sometimes even my mind.

Aching.

Throbbing.

Radiating.

Burning, numb, and decayed.

My body, my strength, and my will to live.

Wavering.

Faltering.

Weakened.

Diminished, withered, and worn.

My faith, my hopes, and all my cares.

I am no longer me.

Each move, each thought, each spoken word is of this wretched shell I am forced to maintain.

This package of non-return that I have to withstand.

There is no longer a living being inside of me.

My heart is no more.

My soul also taken that day.

My mind but a pile of twisted nerves that yearn to connect but the paths have been removed.

My body but a heap of flesh and bones with fatal wounds and scars all over.

My strength and will destroyed in that asinine moment.

My faith is only a mere fragment holding on desperately and my only hope is the chance of reuniting one day –
I beg it be soon for my cares lay buried in the ash at the bottom of the mahogany chest that holds my world.

My world.

Gone.

And I as well.

I Think

I do not see you.
I do not hear you.
But I feel you.
I think of you.
I think you are near.
I think you are with me and that is why I think of you.
I think to call you.
I think you are coming home.
I think I will see you soon.
I think I will hear from you.
It feels so real.
Maybe it is my imagination.
Maybe it is just wishful thinking.
Maybe it is because I want it so badly.
It hurts.
Every time I think I feel you.
It hurts.
Overwhelming.
Gut punch.
Can't breathe.
Feel sick.
Feel like passing out.
Catch my breath.
Take a breath.
Don't scream.
Hold it in.
It will pass.
It hurts.
But it's all that I have.

Life

Life takes you by surprise,
bringing you news of good and bad -
taking things away and giving you things you've never had.

Life gives you moments -
some you never want to forget,
and others that you wish were spared that are drenched with horrid regret.

Life takes you places -
hills of strife roaring up and down,
valleys of winding pleasure swirling you all around.

Life is uncertain and there's never a guarantee;
the day could be filled with sunshine and spring
or a downpour of hurricane wintered misery.

Life Is what you make of it, and you often hold the reins -
then other times the steed rips away and throws you from the carriage
with unbearable deadly pain.

Life changes with every passing day,
from the wrinkles to the grays of age, and the seasons showing nature's way.

Life is short and life is unfair, but life is sweet and dear
and of all the contradictories,
I know that life was so much better
when Caleb was near.

Just a Dream

I think you visit me in my dreams,
I wake up and have recollection of seeing you there.
Sometimes I wake up and it feels so real,
I look around to search for you everywhere.
Sometimes it's just seeing your face and when I wake up I don't recall what was said;
other times we are living life or laying together and loving in our bed.
There's been a few that were not that nice,
memories of arguments or fights; there's been one or two where I was mad-
those are the ones I wish I never had.
Some make no sense, and I can't figure them out,
and a few times I wake and can't remember what they were about.
There's been a few that I've woken up to with great peace,
feeling your presence as if you were holding me through the night as I was asleep.
With each dream I have
there always comes tears,
because it reminds me of the pain
of not having you here.
They say dreams have meanings and a dream is a wish,
and we all know the wish of my heart -
so it's killing me to know they are only just a dream -
you are still gone, and my heart is torn apart.
Please come each night and visit me in my dreams,
I know it's just a dream but it's better than nothing;
it's an escape from the nightmares and a chance to be together,
it's just a dream but your love is what it brings.

Without You

I lay here.
I watch our shows.
Season premieres.
Returns.
New episodes.
Time moves forward.
Life continues.
But without you.

I still feel as if you will be home any minute.
I look at my phone, thinking you will call any minute.
Looking for a text.
Checking the tracker.
Wondering how far from home you are.
Overtime.
Extra job.
Picked up a shift.
Finishing a report.
Made an arrest.
Last minute call.
Traffic stop.
Quick stop by the office.
Almost home.
Maybe you're out of town.
At a training.
Conference.
You'll call at the lunch break or in between classes.
You'll call when you get out and again before bed.
You're not really gone.
You can't be.
It just doesn't feel real yet.
It doesn't feel right.
Will it ever?
Am I just in denial?
Am I crazy?

I lay here.
I watch our shows.
Life continues.
But without you.
Everything is now without you.

Questions.

How are you doing?
How's it going?
How've you been feeling?
How are the kids?
How are things?
Do you need help with anything?
Take it one day at a time.
It gets easier.
Things will get better.
Get some rest.
Stay strong.
Keep going.

Answers.

Not good.
Terrible.
Miserable.
Quiet.
Existing.
Yes.
I can only handle moment by moment.
How can that be.
Not possible.
Have to stay busy.
I'm barely hanging on.
When can I give up.

Managing

My world is upside down.
My heart is shattered.
My life is ruined.
My everything is gone.
From morning to night and in between,
I am alone and torn and empty.
I'm doing the best that I can but don't know what to do and have no idea how to cope.
People keep asking me how I am and if there's anything that they can do.
I'm managing, I guess, if that's what I'm doing.
At least I am out of bed.
Keeping life going for the kids and the house but not much more I can take.
Paying the bills. Preparing the meals. Making calls when things go awry. House cleaning, lawn care, repairs, and such -
but that's just the surface.
Managing is all I can manage to manage and help is what I need.
But it's a thorned bundle of aide for there is no real aide and nothing anyone can do to help.
So how am I doing?
　　How are things going?
　　　　Is there anything that I need?
　　　　　　Well, I am managing, I guess, if that's what I'm doing, and you can't give me what I need.

Til Death Do Us Both Depart

When I see you again,
we'll be together again,
and this time it will be forever.
No one and nothing will separate us again,
and we'll have eternity then.
Dancing and singing and holding each other in a beautiful paradise.
No interruptions, no canceled dates, money will not be an issue anymore.
Time will mean nothing - we'll have plenty of time and all the time to spend time together.
Get everything ready and wait for me, baby - be watching for me when I arrive.
Open the gate and clear the crowds,
because I will come running.
I will jump in your arms and hold on so tight - I will never let go this time.
But until that day comes,
just watch over us and stop by when you can.
Send me a sign or a message of sorts to let me know you're here.
I'll be watching out for you and waiting for your visit and hoping they come often.
I know you've got work to do up there,
so I understand it could be long.
But try and hurry down as soon as you can,
and I'll be here when you come.
I know I won't hear you,
I may not feel your touch,
and I know I won't see your face,
but when I do see you again,
we'll be together again,
and this time it will be forever.

People Watching

Watching people walk by and people around,
at the stores, at dinner, around town.
Couples and families and people living life,
children laughing, friends talking, the love of a husband and wife.
Family dinners, celebrations, life's daily chores,
enjoying the day, or going to school or to work,
hanging out, making memories, spending time together,
some with no care in the world.
Couples on a date - one's been married for years and the other showing off their new baby girl.
People all around with joy on their face,
people all around enjoying their days.
People all around with their loved ones near,
but some don't appreciate it and hold their blessings dear.
It doesn't make sense, it's not right, it just isn't fair –
why do I have to suffer and lose my everything and they don't even care.
On their phones, complaining, ignoring their time,
and I have to sit here without the love of mine.
They take it for granted, they don't even try,
I just sit here and watch these people walk by.
I sit here and watch these people with all this anger inside,
I listen to the complaints and my pain I hide.
It doesn't make sense, it's not right, it just isn't fair -
watching people walk by, watching people live life.

The Double-Edged Sword Gets Sharper

I can't stay home all day alone,
it's taking too much of a toll,
but I can't get out of bed some days and just don't want to face the world.

I stay busy and distracted so that the pain is controlled,
but then I feel guilty that I didn't give you the thoughts you deserved.

I try to stop the tears and put a hold on crying,
but then I feel it all bottled up inside and my emotions go flying.

I don't want to keep fighting,
my strength is all gone,
but I have to make it through for the kids and keep life moving along.

Your pictures and things are a constant reminder of the absence and misery that surrounds my days,
but seeing your face and holding your belongings is a comfort I need in this endless race.

I know you are gone and to never return,
but I can't help but feel like you are coming home any moment - at least that is what I yearn.

One more day without you is another day of hell,
but one more day without you is another day closer to being with you again as well.

The Truth is Ugly

You are doing great.
You are strong.
You look good.
The house looks great.
The kids are good.
We are proud of you.
You can do this.
We understand.
We are praying for you.
God loves you.
We are here for you.
You are not alone.
I'm barely hanging on.
I want to give up.
I showered finally.
I hired help.
They don't say much.
I have no choice.
I don't want to.
You don't - you can't.
Prayers didn't save my husband.
He let this happen.
You can't really help me.
Caleb is gone.

What Will They Say

In a few months, a few years, in a decade or two, what will they say?

Will they remember the nights I didn't make dinner or the ones I forced myself to get up and prepare something worthwhile?

Will they still think I've gone crazy or that I cried too much?

Will they commend me for not giving up like my own mother did?

Will they recall that I kept the house clean and let them do their own thing?

Will they know that I only cared about their joy and really just wanted to stay in bed all day?

Will they know I hid in the closet so that they wouldn't hear my cries?

Will they know I wanted to talk about him all day, every day, but I didn't want to get upset or make them upset?

Will they know that sometimes I needed to be alone so I could cry and scream and say awful things and I didn't want them to know or see?

Will they know that when I was alone I wanted desperately for them to come and talk to me, lay with me, let me be by their side - I hated that they sat in their rooms and on their phones all night.

When I picked them up, took them here and there, and attended all their events, will they know it was the only thing that kept me alive?

Will they know I dreaded the day they were all grown and gone - feared the day when I would be alone for good?

In a few months, a few years, a decade or two, what will they say?

Will they say I made the right choices even though I doubted every single thing I did?

Will they even understand?

Will they even know or care?

Will they remember any of these days or will it be too painful so they block it all out?

In a few months will it still be this bad?

In a few years will things be easier, better, or just different?

In a decade or two will we still talk about him?

Will we say his name?

Will we even remember him - really, truly remember him?

Will I keep myself feeling this way so that I don't forget him?

Will I stop crying every day - or will I force myself to continue as a means of not being "ok" - because when I'm "ok" it means he's really gone.

Will they remember how miserable I was or will they say I did the best I could and that I was there for them?

In a few months, a few years, a decade or two, what will they say?

What will anyone say?

Will there be anyone left to say anything and will I be here to hear

His Family

Maybe they are pretending, hiding it, or trying to stay strong.
Maybe that's how they grieve.
Maybe they just have more faith and see life and death differently.
I know they do.
They seem so happy.
Husband and wife. Kids.
Happy families.
Smiles. Laughs.
Living life.
Moving forward. Moving on.
Date nights. Family functions. Celebrations.
And so forth.
Prayers. Church. God's blessings.
God is good. Thank you, Jesus.
How.
I'm a third wheel.
Obviously alone.
Singled out.
Uncomfortable.
I just don't understand.
How can they pretend.
How can they be okay.
How can they keep moving forward.
How can they find joy.
How can they thank God for this.
God allowed this.
God did this.
Their prayers didn't work.
How can they be ok.

Empty Chair

Set a plate there.
But no one can sit there.
Leave that spot empty -
don't waste a plate.
No one is going to sit there anyways.
That's just an Empty Chair.
Talk about him.
But don't get upset.
Try to join in.
But stay silent.
Look around at the families.
See the Empty Chair.
Say grace. Say thanks.
Useless prayers. Nothing to be thankful for.
Jokes. Conversations. Stories. Memories.
But there's no real smiles or laughter.
There's just an Empty Chair.
It doesn't matter what time we eat.
It doesn't matter whose house we're at.
It doesn't matter what's on the menu.
It doesn't matter who all attends.
There will still be an Empty Chair.
There will always be an Empty Chair.
I want to throw the Empty Chair out the window.
I want to crush it into a million pieces.
I want to see it ignite into flames in the back yard.
I hate the Empty Chair.
I want to fill the Empty Chair.
You should be in that Empty Chair.
Leave the Empty Chair.
Forever an Empty Chair.

All Around Me

Joyful smiles.

Family photos.

Playing with the kids.

Showing off new beginnings, milestones, and gatherings.

Trips to town, to the beach, fun times, and happy days.

Date nights, vacations, movie night, family dinners, getaways.

Holding hands, hugs, heads on shoulders, loved ones and friends.

It's as if they have all forgotten that his life had an end.

Not just a passing of life, not just the way it is, not the circle of life.

Tragic and awful and not fair, God is good is a lie.

The sun is not shining, it's not a great day.

This is not how our story was supposed to go - this is not the way.

All I can do is ignore them, look away, keep scrolling, wipe the tears away.

Force a grin, say "that's cool," make up an excuse, pretend - that's how I spend my days.

Six Months

Half a year.
Six months.
26 weeks.
184 days.
4,416 hours.
264,960 minutes.
15,897,600 seconds.
Of pain,
Of misery,
Of anguish,
Of loneliness,
Of anger,
Of guilt,
Of regret,
Of tears,
Of emptiness,
Of grief,
Of fear,
Of worry,
Of questions,
Of unknowingness,
Of uncertainty,
Of suffering,
Of affliction,
Of agony,
Of torture,
Of numbness,
Of exertion,
Of strain,
Of hopelessness,
Of heart wrenching, wretched brokenness.
Endless.
Yet, they say time heals all wounds...
It's been six months without you.
I still feel like you're coming home.
It still doesn't feel real.
Six months.
Half a year.
Six months is nothing compared to our time together...
We knew each other for 25 years.
We had almost twenty years of love and life.
Six months isn't that long.
Yet even a zeptosecond without you is too much.

Don't

How can they say "God is good"?
How can they say "with God's grace"?
How can they say "Jesus loves"?
How can they say "Gods comfort"?
How can they celebrate?
How can they smile and laugh?
How can they find joy?
How can they move forward?
Look around!! Caleb is gone!!!
Am I being selfish?
Am I stuck in grief?
Am I crazy?
Are they just hiding, pretending?
Are they just grieving differently?
Do they really have that much faith that Caleb being killed can just be shrugged off as a "terrible accident"?
I am falling apart.
I am so broken and angry, I can't see straight.
I want to scream.
I want to break things.
I want the people responsible for this "mistake" to suffer.
To pay.
To admit fault.
To do better.
I don't want to gather with the family and celebrate.
I don't want to have dinners.
I don't want to take photos.
I don't want any of this!

A Brief Moment

I woke up today and for a brief moment,
everything felt "normal."
I didn't realize you were gone.
It didn't feel like you were gone.
It's as if I could have rolled over and you would be
laying there.
It's as if I could have gotten up and looked for you or
called you.
It's as if I forgot all about these last six months.
It's as if I had woke up and it was all over.
Back to normal.
For a brief moment.
Then the moment was over and I remembered you
were gone.
I felt the emptiness.
It hurt because I couldn't believe my mind would play
such a cruel trick.
It hurt because I couldn't believe I could forget so
easily.
It hurt because I knew the normality of the moment
was false.
It hurt because the normality of the moment was
over, ended.
For a brief moment, I felt nothing.
Thought nothing.
I woke up, looked at my phone, saw the time.
I slept in.
It was later than I thought.
I checked an email.
Checked a missed text.
Started to scroll thru for the other notifications of what
I had missed thru the early morning hours.
It felt like any other day.
Any other Sunday.
I almost started to wonder what the schedule would
be for the day.
I almost thought to ask you.
I almost thought you were there.
For a brief moment, things were how they should be.
For a brief moment.
For a brief moment, maybe you were here.

Maybe that's why I didn't think anything of it.
Maybe that's why it was "normal."
Maybe that's why I forgot or didn't realize what life
was like now.
Maybe that's why I just thought it was any other day.
Maybe you were beside me.
Maybe you are still beside me as I write this.
As I cry.
As I fill with pain.
As my stomach turns with knots.
As my body goes numb.
As my mind crumbles and my heart aches with
loneliness.
Maybe you are here.
I imagine you laying here.
Beside me.
Laying on your back, arms and hands pulled slightly
on your chest.
Head turned just to the side.
Just enough that I can see you and steal a kiss.
Maybe you are letting out a little snore.
I look over.
I laugh. I roll my eyes.
I nudge you as it gets louder.
You catch your breath, groan, whisper, "sorry."
Then you turn over. Face the fan and go right back to
sleep.
I scoot over closer to you.
Snuggle up against your back.
I can't really put my arms around you, but I try.
I pull you in closer.
I hold on tight.
For a brief moment, I feel you.
But then I remember you are gone and I hold on
tighter.
I don't want to let go.
Please. Don't take him away again.
Please. Let him stay.
Let me hold onto him and never let go. Please.
For a brief moment.
Let me have a brief moment.

Six vs Five

Everything we have is for a family of six.
Bought a car that can fit six.
Six cups came with the pitcher.
We have six blue bowls and six holiday cups.
We have six mugs for hot cocoa.
Six ice cream bowls.
A couch with six places to sit.
Six stocking hangers for our six stockings.
An ornament with six snowmen.
Six chairs on the back porch.
They even make a pack of six toothbrushes.
There are tables for six.
Or there's a two and a four we can scoot together or an eight and we can spread out a little.
Six can fit just fine in a large booth.
You can get a family deal for four and add a package for two.
Six is perfect.
There's no one stuck in the middle.
No one left out.
Everyone always has a partner.
Everyone always has a pair.
Six is a good number.
Six is even.
Six is complete.
Five is not.
Now someone is left out.
Now someone is in the middle.
Now there's an empty spot everywhere we go.
Now one thing is left behind every time.
Now it's a pack of four and add only one.
Now it's odd.
Odd is not normal.
Odd is not right.
Odd isn't what it's supposed to be.
Odd isn't acceptable.
Odd isn't what we want.
We want six.
We don't want five.
Six.
Not five.
Six.

Sunday Calls

Annie calls on Sundays.
When she gets the privilege at least.
She's only missed a couple so far.
Most calls are thirty minutes long.
A few have been more.
Sometimes service works and she can FaceTime or send me a photo.
I look forward to her Sunday calls.
I think all week towards Sunday.
I write her every day and get a few letters from her too, but Sunday calls are the best.
I used to look forward to Tuesdays because it was your night off and we would get to spend time together in the evening and you would be with me at night.
And on Wednesdays, you wouldn't be as tired and we would stay up late and sometimes have a little date night. Even if it was just watching tv together. We had a really great last Wednesday together.
I hated Thursdays because you worked all day and went back to work at night. I barely saw you on Thursdays. I only saw you for about 15 minutes on our last Thursday together.
I no longer have those days.
Now I wait for Sunday calls from Annie.
I would really like a Sunday call from you.
I wish Heaven had Sunday calls.

Hello. Goodbye.

When someone says hello,
you intend on a goodbye,
a see you later, until next time,
talk to you soon.

When you leave for the day,
run to town, or go to work,
you intend to return, to be home later, to come back soon.

-He went to work that morning,
said goodbye and kissed us kids, double shift and stuff going on after work, be home late,
but we intended for him to return, to be home later, to come back soon.

-She went out for the day, to enjoy some time at the park, said goodbye as we left for school;
she even called again later and said "I love you."
We intended for her to return, to be home later, to come back soon.

-He left for an extra job earlier that day, just a short shift, so a quick kiss to all and "I'll see you guys
later." Several things to do that evening and everyone coming and going, paths crossed quickly, lots
to do, so "I'll call you later." Running late, gotta go, but two days off for the busy weekend, be home
in the morning. We intended for him to return, to be home later, to come back soon.

But he didn't return,
she wasn't home later,
he never came back.

Not all hellos get a proper goodbye,
and some none at all.

Not OK

People say it gets easier.
People say I'll be ok.
People say I can keep going.
People say I am strong.

But the reality is,
I fake a smile.
I force a conversation.
I have to drag myself outside.
I push my empty, broken body along.
I make myself live despite the agony and constant torturous affliction I endure every moment of the day.
How anyone who has lost the love of their life has managed to get through this, is a wonderment to me.
One more day without you is one more day closer to being with you again.
Or at least I beg and plead that is true.
The only way I survive is thru the hope that we will reunite one day.
The only way I carry on is thru the thought that you are out there waiting for me.
The only way I fare this world without you is thru the fragment of faith that you surround me and have your arms around me as I crumble and weep.

I am in Hell. Constant, living Hell.
When will it end?
When will I feel relief?
Peace?
Freedom?

But if that day comes, does that mean I am ok that you are gone?
Does that mean you are forgotten?
Does that mean I have moved on?
Moved forward?
Do I want that day to come?
How can I be ok not being ok?
How can I live without you?
How can this ever be ok?
How can I let go but keep you still?
How can I get thru this pain.
This emptiness. This loneliness.

Maybe the truth is, I don't want to.
Maybe the truth is, I can't.
Maybe the truth is, I never will.

Is it ok to be ok?
How can it be?

It's not ok to not have you.
Losing you is not ok.

I am not ok.

Second Chances.

If I could go back,
I would love harder.
Stronger.
Longer.
I would talk more.
Hug more.
Hold hands more.
Kiss more.
Love more.
I would listen.
Linger on every word.
Love every word.
Spend more time together.
Truly together.
Forgive.
Forget.
Appreciate and value.
Give in.
Compromise.
Just let it be.
Watch your choice of show.
Leave the radio station on.
Let you play guitar for hours.
Hold on more.
Hold on tighter.
Hold on longer.
Show you every day in every way how important you are.
How special you are.
How loved you are.
Wanted.
Desired.
Needed.
Loved in every way.
From top to bottom.
Inside and out.
I would do so many things differently.
Do better.
Be better.
If I had a second chance.
A do-over.
If I could go back.

Tired

I sit.
I cry.
I scream with grief.
I look around, desperate for relief.
Some peace.
Comfort.
Who can I call.
Who can come.
No one can ease the pain.
Pray, they say. Ask for God's comfort.
Talk to a counselor, they say. Talking about it helps.
Journal, they say. Get it all out.
Call someone who understands, they say. They can give you advice.
Call a friend or loved one, they say. They can come and sit with you.
But talking to the sky doesn't help.
Talking to a stranger doesn't help.
Writing it out doesn't help.
Advice won't help.
And no one understands.
What will help?
Time?
Time stands still in my heart and in my soul.
Time runs empty as my tears flood the room.
Time mocks me as I sit alone thru the hours.
I'm tired.
I'm worn.
I'm reaching desperation.
All I can do is sit and cry.
Wishing you were here.
All I can do is sit and wipe away my tears.
Wash my face.
Breathe and push through.
I have no choice.
But I'm tired.

Waiting

Waiting on the courts -

Waiting on the defense -

Waiting on the truth -

Waiting for your belongings -

Waiting for answers -

Waiting for paperwork -

Waiting on people to do their jobs -

Waiting on people to reply, respond -

Waiting to find out what the outcomes will be -

Waiting for benefits for the kids -

Waiting on dates for events -

Waiting to see if events will happen -

Waiting for covid to end so events can happen, -

so court can happen, -

so answers can happen, -

so time can continue -

Waiting for peace -

Waiting for time to heal -

Waiting on a sign, -

a message, -

a signal -

Waiting for you to call -

Waiting on you to walk in the door -

Waiting for this all to be over -

Waiting for the days to end -

Waiting for us to be together again -

Waiting on the guilt and regrets to fade, -

pass by, -

end -

Waiting to see if that is possible -

Waiting to see if any of this is possible -

Waiting -

Waiting –

Wishing –

89

Honor Wall

At attention.
Salute.
Straight ahead.
Don't flinch.
Ignore the sweat.
Ignore the tears.
Ignore the cries as the wife and kids walk through.
Don't let it get to you - I know it's hard.
Avoid eye contact - it will make it harder.
Don't lock your knees.
Keep it together.
Stay strong.
Stay tough.
Breathe.
It may be hot.
It may be cold.
It may rain.
It may snow.
Inside.
Outside.
Hundreds lined up.
Feels like miles.
Feels like strength.
Feels like pride.
Feels like family.
Class As - all different colors.
All coming together.
All for one purpose.
One mission.
Honor wall.
Honor the fallen.

Don't – Can't - Must

Chairs are set up.
The stage is prepared.
Photos and treasures on display.
Flowers arranged.
Schedule is made.
Speeches written.
Music is in order.
Slideshow has been turned in.
Everything looks beautiful.
Everything looks honorable.
It's time to get dressed.
It's time to get ready.
Fix your hair.
Look nice.
Pretty dress.
Button shirt, slacks, belt.
Dress shoes.
Jewelry.
Don't forget your ribbon.
Everyone looks so nice.
You would say I looked beautiful.
It would have made me smile.
I wanted to be beautiful for you.
I felt beautiful for you.
I wanted everything beautiful for you.
Honor you.
All is put together, yet I'm falling apart.
I don't want to do this.
This isn't right.
Not how it should be.
I don't want to do this.
I don't know if I can do this.
Escorts are here.
The family car arrives.
The drive is short yet so far away.
Cars line the highways and roads.
Traffic is backed up.
So many people.
So overwhelming.
Patrol cars, fire engines, flags.
We drive under Old Glory.
Hanging from the ladders.
Waving.

Welcoming.
Honorable.
Officers line the driveway.
An honor wall of blue yet with different colors but all the same.
Class As.
Ties.
Hats.
Gloves.
From near and far.
All close together.
All one family.
Saluting.
Standing proudly.
Standing with sorrow.
Many close friends.
Familiar faces.
Tears in their eyes.
Some who are strangers, yet the pain is still present.
A sight to see.
A sight to respect.
A sight full of pride.
Too many to thank.
You would've said hello to each and every one.
Shared a story or two.
Exchanged numbers.
Strangers yet friends.
Now family.
The car stops.
We file out.
Take a deep breath.
Chin up.
Hold the kids close.
I don't want to do this.
I don't know if I can do this.
The honor wall continues.
The room is overflowing.
People outside.
People standing.
All around and on the sides.
The honor wall lines the aisle.
Guiding me towards my final goodbye.

Photos, songs, beautiful words.
Remembering.
Honoring.
Final goodbye.
Final touch.
Final kiss.
They move you out.
Move you by.
I want to hold on.
Block the path.
Make them go away.
Make it all go away.
I don't want to do this.
I don't think I can do this.
One last song.
The song of goodbye.
I really don't want to do this.
Tears.
Cries.
Screams of pain.
More salutes.
21 goodbyes.
A jump with each boom.
Tears.
Cries.
Screams of pain.
Flags folded tightly.
Final call.
Answer the radio.
Pick up.
Respond.
Tears.
Cries.
Screams of pain.
Taking you away.
Pushing you further away.
Taking you away.
Come back.
Come back.
Come back.
You are gone.
I don't want to do this.
I don't want to do this.
I don't want to do this.
I can't do this.

But

Talking about you feels good.
But
Talking about you makes me sad.

Thinking about you brings smiles.
But
Thinking about you brings tears.

"Talking to you" makes me feel like you're close by.
But
"Talking to you" makes me feel like you're so far away.

Writing expresses the pain.
But
Writing fuels the pain.

Sleeping distracts.
But
Sleeping ignores.

Our love is still present.
But
Our love is in the past.

You are my husband.
But
I can't check married.

There are things to be said.
But
You don't say anything back.

I feel you.
But
I can't find you.

I want you.
But
I can't have you.

I need you.
But
You are gone.
—————————————————————

I Miss You

I miss your eyes.
Deep blue.
Safe.
Beautiful.
Pulled me in.
Site of love.

I miss your hands.
Soft but firm.
Safe.
Gentle.
Intertwined with mine.
Point of love.

I miss your arms.
Strong and open.
Safe.
Inviting.
Held me close.
Place of love.

I miss your kiss.
Sweet.
Safe.
Intoxicating.
Delicate.
Sharing of love.

I miss your voice.
Loud.
Safe.
Comforting.
Gave me joy.
Tone of love.

I miss your laugh.
Booming.
Safe.
Goofy and fun.
Gave me smiles.
Sound of love.

I miss your knowledge.
Abundant.
Safe.
Overzealous.
Kept me in awe.
One of the many things I love.

I miss your talents.
Plethora.
Safe.
Impressive.
Music and more.
Love beyond love.

I miss hearing Sinatra in the kitchen while you cooked.

I miss your ridiculous shows that drove me crazy.

I miss you leaving all the lights on and saying you're about to go back in there.

I miss you playing guitar and piano - any song you can think of.

I miss you making a mess in the bathroom sink and long luxurious baths.

I miss secret texts and Facebook messages and midday and midnight calls.

I miss doing projects and events and adventures with you.

I miss spending life with you.

I miss sharing love with you.

I miss everything about you.

Truth

I didn't "lose you."
I'm not suffering from a "loss."
This isn't a game with winners and losers and a dice that you have to toss.

You haven't "passed," "passed on," or "passed away."
You're not a plane that has "departed" and will return another day.

"Deceased" sounds so unnatural and please don't say "demised,"
and if I hear "you're in a better place," I just might lose my mind.

"Resting in eternal peace" is ridiculous and just not right,
and it's stupid to say "you lost the battle" or that you "lost the fight."

All these euphemisms sound like a sham,
and telling me "you didn't make it" sounds like you had other plans.

No matter how you say it, the pain will never go;
don't try and be gentle about it in an attempt to soften the blow.

"God's purpose or plan" is a cruel and twisted lie,
and He didn't "need you" more than we do - there's just no reason why.

You are gone, no longer here, and never will be again;
you were killed by the asinine carelessness of cowardly and lazy men.

This never should have happened; it is a beyond horrible mistake.
Stop calling it a "tragic accident" as if that helps take away the ache.

Nothing anyone can say or do will make me feel any better.
The only cure for this dreadful pain is for us to again be together.
But that cannot and will never be; there's no cure for this agony.
I will forever be frozen in this hellacious and excruciating tragedy.

Constant Realizations

My flesh desires for your touch,
your gentle kiss upon my neck.
Your strong arms wrapped around me, our bodies connecting deep within.
My heart aches for your voice,
your words bringing comfort to my pain.
Your laugh that filled the room and your knowledge that you gave.
My soul yearns for your spirit,
your presence is all I wish.
Your absence is a constant void and has caused my heart to rip,
to shred, to burn, to wither away, broken and shattered on the ground -
I'm in a state of constant suffocation, gasping for air as I drown.
No longer will I feel your touch,
the peace of your embrace.
No longer will I hear your voice,
causing my heart to race.
Your spirit feels so far away and yet I sense your presence.
I long for the day our souls reunite as I'm welcomed into the heavens.
Open the gate, clear the way, and be ready as I arrive.
Until that day I will push on even though I no longer feel alive.
The truth is I died with you that night, yet I didn't see the light.
My heart still beats, my body still moves, I still show signs of life,
but my spirit has forever perished and is no longer truly living inside.
I desire, I ache, I yearn to have you back again,
and until that day comes, I will forever endure this endless strife and pain.

The 29th

I woke up this morning, having dreamt of you.
It felt like a subconscious memory or reality.
Maybe it was a visit,
maybe it was just my imagination-
either way, I woke up feeling numb.
Not sure what was real.
Not even thinking of the day,
but fully aware of what the date was.
I looked at your picture.
I talked to you.
I thought of the sequence of events on that last
Thursday the 28th;
yesterday was Thursday the 28th.
I was coming home from yet another rehearsal, late.
I pretended to call you,
thought about what we would've said,
thought about what we last had said,
thought of the sequence of events of that evening,
that night, the morning, and day,
and the days to come.
Strangely, no tears flowed.
I felt nothing.
I thought to myself,
"I should be a mess."
I didn't understand why I had no feeling -
maybe my brain is trying to take over,
to calm me, to protect me, to keep me sane.
I hate this feeling of getting used to things -
of finding a new normal, a new routine.
I hate this feeling of settling in. It feels like forgetting.
It feels like I'm on the verge of your pictures just being
all I have left.
I already look at your pictures and wonder if that's
really what you looked like -
searching desperately in the back corners of my mind
for a thought,
an image that's real and not a memory, not from a
photograph -
of real time existence.
Frantically thinking of times we spent together,
things we said or did,
thinking of things you liked,
rolling over in the bed and imagining you laying there,
closing my eyes.
I'm trying so hard to pretend like I can hear you –
for real -
like I could feel you.

Sometimes the sensation is overwhelming and I wonder
if your spirit really is here -
other times I scream out in desperation,
begging for a sign,
hoping I'll see something that makes me know your
presence is near.
I never get an obvious message and then I doubt
myself.
I believe in the abilities of the supernatural.
I feel this gut-wrenching stabbing deep within that
you're trying to make contact,
like you're reaching out to talk to me,
and I feel like it could happen,
but I hate that it hasn't yet,
and I wonder what is wrong with me.
I doubt everything I knew, everything we had.
I try to drown out any sad times, fights, or arguments,
rough times throughout our 20 years.
I try to lasso in the happy times,
the moments of true, deep passion and love,
the moments when we thought to our self, "I sure
hope other people in this world are as happy as us,
because it wouldn't be fair for only us to have this kind
of love."
I remember what it feels like to kiss you and hold your
hand.
I remember what it feels like to have you grab me and
hold me,
to come up from behind and wrap your arms around
me so tightly.
I try and find that feeling again and then I wonder if it's
just my imagination or if I'm really feeling it.
Some days I can't stop crying, screaming, angry.
This is not fair.
You should be here.
Why? What did we do wrong?
Why do have to endure this suffering,
this punishment, this cruel torture?
Jealous, envious of other people who got a miracle,
who fought through, who made it, who survived.
Why couldn't we have gotten a miracle?
The entire drive to the hospital I tried to use the power
of prayer, the power of belief -
but you were already gone.
They were a fruitless waste of thoughts and prayers.
All my prayers, all these years - a waste.
Why start now?

There's nothing more to need.
My everything is gone,
and forever more the 29th of every month will be a reminder that my love is gone.
My joy nevermore.
The guilt, the regret, forever ripping inside of me.
And as more and more months pass by,
as years come through and the realities sink in,
I will wake up and not feel - just as I did today.
I will wake and have no tears -just as I did today.
I will wake and eventually you will be gone - completely.

Falling Apart

Sheetrock crumbling and paint chipping away.
Old damage from leaks and floods.
Roof repairs.
Broken appliances.
Water heater went out.
Garbage disposal needs to be replaced.
Timer on the dryer, filter on the washer.
One thing after another.
The house is Falling Apart.
Weeds and grass overgrown.
Flat tire. Dead battery. Mower won't start.
Flowers ruined from the winter nights.
Flower beds look a mess.
The yard is Falling Apart.
Kids in trouble.
Grades dropping.
Attitudes rising.
Pressures of the world.
Lies.
Hiding things.
Wrong choices. Bad choices.
Can't help them. Can't fix them. Can't make them better. Can't be who you were to them.
The family is Falling Apart.
You were the glue.
The tape.
The bond.
The reason for our joy.
For our everything.
You were everything.
Even when everything felt like nothing and the world was Falling Apart, you caught us.
Right into your arms.
Every time.
Now where do we turn?
What do we do?
Who will catch us as the world falls apart?
How do we stop Falling Apart?
Everything is Falling Apart.

I Lay Here

I lay here.
Thinking of you.
Crying for you.
Wishing you were here.
Imagining that you are.
Holding my hand.
Looking into your eyes.
Hearing you laugh.
Your crooked little smile.
Your silly jokes. Irritating.
But comforting.

I lay here.
Missing you.
Alone.
No one to talk to you.
No one to lay with.
My everything gone.
Needing you.
To be held.
To be kissed.
To be loved.

I lay here.
I talk to you.
I beg for an answer.
I pretend you are here.
I think of what it would be like at
this moment if you were still here.
What would we be doing.
Wednesday night.
Your night off.
Night full of shows that I like.
I know you never really wanted to
watch them but you did.   Sort of.
You stayed distracted by your phone
instead.
I should have turned off the tv.
Focused on each other instead.

I lay here.
Wishing we had more time.
Regretting all the wasted time.
Regretting so much.
Feeling guilt.
Feeling anger.
Sadness.
Pain.

I lay here.
Wondering why this happened.
What did I do wrong to deserve this
torture.
What could have been done
differently to stop this.
What went wrong.
What could they have done
differently.
Better.
Faster.

I lay here.
Wanting you.
Missing you.
Needing you.

I lay here.
Alone.
Forever more.
Alone.

I lay here.
You should be laying here, too.

How

How do I get answers when they won't tell me the whole story?

How do I get justice when they have an excuse for everything?

How do I force change when they won't tell me the truth?

How do I make people listen when I don't know what to say?
How do I get help when I don't know who to ask?

How do I help our children when nothing will really help?

How do I manage and battle and get thru this when I can't do this alone?

How do I stay strong when I'm so tired and weak?

How do I find peace when there's no end in sight?

How do I keep living when I'm dead on the inside?

How do I put my life back together when everything is shattered in pieces on the ground?

How do I live without you when I don't know how to do anything?

How?

The Only One

I know I'm not the only one to have ever suffered a loss.
There are more like me.

I know I'm not the only one to have ever felt the pain of grief.
There are more like me.

I know I'm not the only one to have ever become a widow.
There are more like me.

I know I'm not the only one to have to become a solo parent.
There are more like me.

I know I'm not the only one to have to start life over alone.
There are more like me.

I know I'm not the only one to have to do things on their own.
There are more like me.

I know I'm not the only one,
but -
Caleb was my only one,
and there are no more like Caleb and me.

Pieces Left Behind

Doorbell rings.
Dogs barking.
Middle of the night.
Who could it be?
Lock not opening?
Coming home early?
Why didn't you call instead of ringing the bell?
A piece of me was left behind as I heard the bell that night.
Turn the corner.
Lights shining thru the window.
Recognize those colors.
Heart skips a beat.
Forget how to breathe.
Stomach drops.
I know what this means.
You're warned of this moment.
You fear this moment.
You try not to imagine this moment.
You aren't prepared for this moment.
No blue wife ever wants this moment.
Lights shining on the wall.
Fear on the wall.
A piece of me was left behind as I saw the lights on the wall that night.
Open the door.
Two uniforms.
Head of the agency.
Patrol cars in the driveway.
Please.
No.
Let it be something small.
Something minor.
Just a little bit of trouble.
A piece of me was left behind as I opened the door that night.
"I don't like seeing you at my door at 3:30 in the morning."
His shoulders drop.
He gives me the look.
I don't like this.
I know what this means.
A piece of me was left behind as I stood on the porch that night.

"Caleb's been shot.
I need to take you to the hospital."
My legs stop working.
I fall into the door.
The other one catches me.
I can't speak.
No.
I can't breathe.
My kids.
They've awakened.
They're standing in the hall.
They too know what this means.
No.
I can't.
A piece of me was left behind as I heard those words that night.
Get dressed.
Drive to the hospital.
Leave the kids.
An officer is with them.
Another is on the way.
On the way to the house.
Lonely house.
Empty house.
House full of fear.
House full of dread.
Roads are empty.
Nearly 4 in the morning.
People sleeping.
Dreaming.
I should be home.
Sleeping.
Dreaming.
Shouldn't be in this car.
Car of doom.
Car of loneliness.
Cold.
Empty.
Must drive faster.
Why aren't they driving faster?
Please.
Let him be okay.
What happened?
How could this happen?
Are you kidding me?

How the hell does this happen?
He's gonna be ok.
Keep saying it.
Over and over.
He's gonna be ok.
He's gonna be ok.
Believe it.
Speak it.
Pray.
Pray.
Believe.
He's gonna be ok.
Drive faster.
A piece of me was left behind as I rode in the car that night.
Exit.
Turn.
Turn.
Turn.
Stop.
Exit the car.
Slow walk.
Have to remember how to walk.
Tears.
Cold.
Door opens.
People waiting.
Expecting me.
Escorts.
Long hallways.
Cold hallways.
Quiet hallways.
White walls.
White floors.
White coats.
A piece of me was left behind as I entered that place that night.
Empty room.
Waiting.
Waiting.
Waiting.
More uniforms arrive.
Familiar faces.
New faces.
Empty faces.
Fearful faces.
No one is saying anything.
No one is telling me anything.
People leaving.
People entering.

People standing around.
People outside the door.
Waiting.
A piece of me was left behind as I waited that night.
Cold.
Waiting.
Alone.
Waiting.
White coat enters the room.
Doctor and a nurse.
It can't be.
Please.
No.
Cardiac arrest.
"Couldn't bring him back."
No.
Chair goes back.
Fall to the floor.
Screams.
Screams.
Screams.
Bad dream.
Wake up.
Hitting the wall.
Hitting the floor.
Hitting my head.
Wake up.
Over and over.
Wake up.
No.
Please.
Can't be.
Why didn't you try harder?
Do a better job.
Why didn't you do a better job?
A piece of me was left behind as I lay on the floor that night.
Another escort.
Another hallway.
Another room.
Waiting.
Sitting on the floor.
Can't stand up.
Can't do this.
Don't want to do this.
Waiting.
People entering.
People exiting.
A few more minutes.
Let me go in.

Waiting.
A piece of me was left behind as I sat outside that room that night.
Door opens slowly.
Like a dream.
Small room.
Lots of uniforms.
Cabinet.
Desk.
Dr. Red Duke's room.
Legacy.
Honor.
I hate this room.
Uniforms.
Cameras.
Portfolios.
Notebooks.
Circling the room.
Bed in the center.
Flag draped over.
Tubes still intact.
Remove them.
Let me kiss him.
I want to kiss him.
He doesn't need the tubes anymore.
Useless.
Dried blood.
I want to kiss him.
Eyes closed.
Open your eyes.
Touch his forehead.
Touch his cheek.
Tears drop on the flag.
Tears drop on his face.
Wake up.
Uncover him.
Let me touch him.
I feel his hand underneath.
Just pull out his hand.
Hold his hand.
They won't let me kiss his lips.
They won't let me touch his hand.
Useless pleas.
Why didn't I just do it anyways?
Screams.
Screams.
Screams.
Wake up.
Wake up.
Cold.
Wake up.

No.
No.
No.
I don't want to leave.
But I can't stay.
Where do I go anyways?
What do I do now?
I don't want to leave.
No reason to stay.
Useless.
I don't want to leave.
A piece of me was left behind on that flag covered bed that night.
Long walk out.
Numb.
Silent.
Empty.
Lonely.
My heart beats no more.
I breathe no more.
I am no more.
I am forever in that room.
Forever with him.
I never left that room.
Who I am now is not who I was.
Now will I ever be again.
A piece of me was left behind in the hallway that night.
Long drive home.
Phone calls.
Lots of calls.
No words.
Can't find the words.
Don't want to say those words.
News has been shared by now.
Phone calls coming in.
Tears.
Endless tears.
How do I tell them?
What do I say?
How do I go on?
How?
Why?
No.
Why do I have to do this?
Prayers.
Useless prayers.
Believer.
Speak it into power.
Useless.
No wonder they didn't drive faster.
No point.

No rush.
He was gone long ago.
Before they even arrived.
Cold.
Dark.
Empty.
Night.
Night is no more.
Sun has risen but he has fallen.
Never.
No more.
Forever.
Gone.
He.

And I.
Us.
Gone.
Forever.
No more.
A piece of me was left behind that night.
A piece of me was left behind.
So many pieces.
What more is left.
There is no more.
No more pieces left.
No more.
I was left behind with you that night.

In Five Years

In five years, the kids will be graduated, moving out, on to college, on their own.

In five years, it would be just you and me.

In five years, the house will be quiet, empty, no interruptions, no distractions, no more busy activities.

In five years, it would be just you and me.

In five years, we would go on trips, vacations, lots of dates, more money, more time.

In five years, it would be just you and me.

In five years, we would have no excuses, no reasons not to do things, go places, be together.

In five years, it would be just you and me.

In five years, we would start our new life together, full of adventure, excitement, new opportunities, lots of love and passion.

In five years, it would be just you and me.

In five years, we would be starting over, starting fresh, getting back time, lost time, a new honeymoon phase, one we never really got, a new form of togetherness, a new outlook of us.

In five years, it would be just you and me.
Lots of kisses, lots of cuddling, lots of movies, dinners, late night shenanigans, lots of crazy lovin' with no reason to have to be quick or quiet.

It five years it would be just you and me.

But, now... in five years...
it will be just me.

Quiet.
Lonely.
Empty.
Dark.

In five years, it will be just me.

Then What?

People keep saying I'm doing great.
People keep saying I can do this.
People keep saying it will get easier.
People keep saying I'm strong.
But.
I don't feel like I'm doing great.
I sit alone all day.
All night.
I have to keep cleaning. so I don't fall apart.
I feel lonely.
I feel discouraged.
I feel lost.
I feel empty.
I'm just doing great at pretending, but I won't be able to pretend forever.
I don't want to do this; I just have no choice.
If I give up, the kids are left even worse than they already are.
If I give up, there's no one to take care of them, take care of things, keep Caleb's memory alive.
If I give up, I risk not being able to be with Caleb again.
I can only do this because I have to, but soon I won't have any choices left.
It's not getting easier.
It's getting harder.
Harder to take care of everything on my own.
Harder to keep quiet about the truth.
Harder to be patient and wait for justice.
Harder to keep my head above water.
Harder to be alone every day.
Every night.
Harder to manage.
Harder to ignore the guilt, the regrets, the unanswered questions, the secrets, the unknown.
Harder to remember.
Soon it will be too hard.
I'm only strong because I have no choice.
I still have all this paperwork.
I still have all the meetings with the courts.
I still don't know the truth, the whole story.
I still haven't seen justice.
I'm not really strong.
I'm really actually weak.
I can barely stand.
Barely breathe.
Barely keep moving.
I'm only strong because there are still so many things left to do, but soon the paperwork will be complete.
The courts will be finished.
The tasks and duties will be complete.
I'm only strong because I have to be for the kids, but soon the kids won't be kids anymore.
I won't have to be strong anymore.
Then what?

What the Books Don't Tell You

Grief is more than five stages.

Grief is more than sadness.

Grief is more than pain.

Grief is never ending.

Grief is unavoidable.

Grief is trauma.

Grief is tragic.

Grief is ugly.

Grief is wearing the same T-shirt and pajama pants for days because you don't have the strength or motivation to leave the house and face the world, so why bother changing into clean clothes if you're at home all day anyways.

Grief is not having the strength or motivation to do the laundry even if you do change.

Grief is dishes in the sink, on the counter, on the bedside table.

Grief is clothes on the floor.

Grief is an accumulation of dust, dirt, and tears filling every crevice and surface of the house, the heart, the soul.

Greece is missed appointments, meetings, parties, and plans.

Grief is last minute cancellations and apologies and excuses.

Grief is unanswered questions, regrets, and guilt.

Grief is a constant unknowing and no way to ever truly gain the knowledge.

Grief is constantly forgetting, not remembering, an inability to focus, process, and comprehend.

Grief is needing help but not being able to ask for help
because the truth is you need help with everything and no one can fix anything.

Grief is paperwork, forms, applications, and documents lining the counter, in stacks,
an over abundance of emails and phone calls to make.

Grief is signature after signature after signature and filling out the same information over and over and over again.

Grief is reliving, replaying, instantly, constantly.

Grief is spending hours staring at photos, watching videos, reading the same messages in a constant
an endless loop, hoping that the photo will come to life, that the video will suddenly be in real time,
that the message will show meaning and be spoken into existence.

Grief is laying on the bathroom floor, sitting in the closet, holding his clothes so tightly.

Grief is touching his toothbrush, his razor, the last things he touched that night.

Grief is constantly looking at the clock knowing exactly what happened at that very moment,
reliving it, dreading it, hoping the clock will stop, skip, reverse and start again.

Grief is not changed through therapy, counseling, or prayer.

Grief cannot seek comfort, peace, closure.

Grief is forcing a smile behind your red, burning eyes and puffy face,
permanently scarred from hours of tears and cries.

Grief is faking an "ok" when people ask you how you're doing.

Grief is hating when people ask you how you're doing - what a stupid question.

Grief is hating being alone but not wanting anyone around - except your husband.

Grief is pretending, acting, false sense of reality, lost identity.

Grief is walking aimlessly around the house from room to room,
through the doorways, around the porch and driveway.

Grief is staring out into the abyss of loneliness –
begging, screaming, pleading for change –
hoping for an answer, a sign, something.

Grief is being unable to remember where you put things, desperately searching,
hoping you will find them and killing yourself over not taking better care of precious things.

Grief is all of the bad thoughts and fears creeping and taking over,
putting your mind into a wretched, fiery pool of paranoia.

Grief is not what they say it is.

Grief is dark.

Grief is empty.

Grief shows no mercy.

Grief finds your weaknesses and torments you with them, taunts you, tortures you.

The books don't tell you the whole story.

Like A Child

I am like a child
lost in a crowded department store,
searching in desperation,
thru the isles, the racks, the shelves, frantic for answers -
why, when, who, what, where....
Alone and aware of the unknown.

Will I ever be found?

Will I ever discover who I am in need of?

Will I come out of this darkness, this wasteland of emptiness, loneliness, confusion and fear?

I am like a child
with no control or independence,
told when to wake, when to sleep, what to do and where to go -
what I can and cannot do, see, say....
Crushed by the power of those over me,
diminished and destroyed.

Will I ever be able to do as I wish,
as I need?

Will I ever be able to stand up and grow, be tall, be strong, be taken seriously, be more than this
child-like persona that has taken over me?

Will I ever be able to know what they know and not be dismissed as a pitiful peasant with a putrid spirit?

I am like a child
sent to his room, closed away, unable to be included.
Excluded by the ones around me.
Told I have to wait, told I have no rights, told to go away.
Shot down, shut down, broken.
Desperate to be, to know, to do,
and punished with inexperience,
lack of knowledge, and naivety.

Will I ever be able to do things on my own?

Will I ever be able to face this world without ridicule, shame, guilt, regret –
without the pressing dominance of my in-existence?

Will I ever be able to return, to be me again, to be anew?

I am like a child.
I am lost.
I am powerless.
I am alone.

When will I be a grown up again?

Promises

To be released from the tears
From the loneliness
From all the fears and lies
To be whole once more
As our hearts are reconciled
Amongst the firmament of paradise.

To be released from the darkness
From the silence
From all that's shattered deep within
To see the sunshine again
As our arms reach out to reunite
Amongst the streets of golden light.

To be released from the regrets
From the guilt
From all the burdens of strife
To have all the unknowns taken away
As our souls are reconnected
Amongst the promise of eternal life.

Chess

Game board.

Four borders.

Boundaries.

Restrictions.

Moved by importance of who you are,
constant unseen defeat,
constant unknown,
constant limitations.

Follow the rules.

Pawns.

Sacrificed.

Pushed around, never settled,
no power,
captured,
destroyed.

Follow the rules.

Check.

Check again.

Checkmate.

No power.
No control.
No way out.

Stuck as a pawn in a game of chess.

A game called life.

Checkmate.

Court Clothes

I have a shirt that hangs in the bathroom, separate from all the other clothes.
It doesn't get tucked away into the closet because it doesn't fit in with the rest.
It doesn't belong.
It hangs precisely without a crinkle, without a sign of wear.
It's not something for daily use, or even when I need to dress nicely.
It has one purpose, and one purpose only.
I only wear it then.

I wear black dress pants with this shirt.
Dress pants that I've had for many years actually.
They are slightly faded and show some wear.
Years of professionalism, formality, and times when a pair of casual jeans would not be appropriate.
I have worn these pants for quite some time and now as I slide them on, they fit differently.
They no longer hug my skin, giving me a sense of self-consciousness.
They are loose and baggy and do not match my silhouette.
Most would say that is a compliment, a sign of fitness and hard work.
Some would say "good job."
However, they are loose now as my body has changed as my life has been forever changed.
It is not the way one should have wanted to lose weight.
I really should get a new pair.

I have an entire regiment of jewelry that goes along with this outfit.
Each piece serves a meaning, symbolism, a story.
I put on each piece.
One at a time.
Fighting back tears as I close each clasp.

As I complete my outfit and take a step to look in the mirror, I ask myself,
"Do I look nice?
Do I look strong?
Do I look confident?
Do I feel empowered?
Can I handle the day ahead of me?"

The truth is -
I can't.
But somehow this outfit allows me to feel like I can face it.
This outfit is a costume for a character I did not audition for, and a role I do not want to accept.
It is my mask, and it's becoming my uniform.
I don't want to wear a uniform.

Restricting.
Constricting.
Controlling.
I hate this outfit.

I wouldn't wear it any other time, so why do I have to now.
I don't want to wear this, but I still put it on.
I have no choice.

Hollow

Empty,

Void,

Barren,

Lifeless,

Vacant,

Cavity,

Unfilled,

Cavern,

Hole,

Pit,

Futile.

Me.

No Stars

—————————— * ——————————

There is a star that sits above the house;
if you look up at the sky right at the end of the sidewalk, you will see it.
It shines differently than all the others.
It sits alone, almost separated, apart from all the other stars around it.
It gives off a glow, not a twinkle.
It shines bright like a porch light, a guide to where you are.
I come outside each night to look for this star.
It feels like it exists only now - for me, from you.
I look up at it and feel you.
I think it is you.
I talk to it.
Well, not really to it exactly, I talk out loud,
but when it is there, I talk to you as if you are there as well.
As if you are there, perched and looking down, looking down and smiling.
I can look up at the sky and immediately find where this star rests.
I don't have to search; I know exactly where it is.
I connect to it immediately, and not just at the end of the sidewalk,
but any time I look up at the sky, I can find it.
I know where it is - I know where you will be.
When the stars are out at night, I feel like you are out at night,
watching and standing guard, patrolling, protecting.
Night shift.

There are no stars tonight.

No signs of life up there.
No twinkling, no wonder, no beauty to abound, no great mystery to behold.
No connection to you or ways of contact.
There are too many clouds tonight.
The stars are too far away tonight, hidden, buried, covered up.
I can't find our star.
But I know that you are still here, looking down, looking down and smiling.
You are still here, watching and standing guard, patrolling, protecting.
Night shift.

—————————— * ——————————

So Many Questions,
So Many Things to Say

What would I say if I could talk to you again?
What would I ask you if I had the chance?
So many questions, so many things to say.
I would ask you if you're okay.
I would ask you if you felt pain, if you were scared, if
you need anything.
I would ask what Heaven is like and if you get to sing
and play guitar all you want.
I would ask you how am I supposed to get through all of
this without you.
I would ask you to talk to the kids, to help them, the
way you always did.
I would ask you to tell me what to do.
I would ask you to tell me "It will all work out. We will
figure it out. We will make it work," the way you
always did.
I would ask you to tell me the truth about all the
unknowns, fears, worries, and paranoias that I have.
I would ask you to explain the things I've learned since
you were taken, the things I have discovered.
I would ask you to explain yourself.
I would ask you for forgiveness.
I would ask you to tell me how to fix things around the
house, how to work things, how to handle things.
I would ask you to get things off the top shelf for me,
to move the heavy things, to wash the pans, to cook
dinner and to listen to Sinatra while you did.
I would ask you to play the piano, the guitar, any
instrument, and I would record you playing so I could
replay it on repeat for all the seconds that I have left to
live without you.
I would ask you to talk, to tell me stories, even if
you've already told them to me before, multiple times.
I would even let you talk as loud as you want and I
wouldn't say anything about it.
I would ask you to take a picture with me.

I would ask you to hold me, to kiss me, to dance with
me, to talk to me, to make love to me.
I would ask you why you had to leave, why it had to be
you, why this had to happen?
I would ask you what God has to say about this, his
explanation, his reason for why he took you from us.
Why did he choose you?
Why not one of the others?
Why did this have to happen at all?
Why didn't he intervene?
Why weren't you spared, saved, sent back, sent home?
I would ask you to please come home.
I would say I'm sorry for all the stupid fights and
arguments and fussing through the years.
I'm sorry for the nagging and complaining that often
comes from a wife.
I'm sorry for criticizing, demanding, or anything
I said or did that negated how much I love you
and how truly valued you are to me.
I'm sorry for pushing you away when I didn't feel like
talking it out, or talking at all, or when I was in a funk, or
not in the mood.
I'm sorry for rejecting you or turning away, for every kiss
or touch I denied you.
I'm sorry for not showing you in every moment, every
day, in every way what an incredibly amazing and
talented, special and priceless gift you are to me.
I'm sorry for ever making you feel less than.
I'm sorry for not listening, giving you a chance, or letting
you be right, first, or heard.
I'm sorry for hogging the tv and the radio, for taking the
bigger counter and closet – the truth is - you needed
the room more than I really did!
I'm sorry for never letting you leave the kitchen cabinet
lights on overnight and griping about the fan bothering
me. (I keep them on now by the way, just for you...I still
think they look bad though.

I moved the fan so it's not blowing directly at me, but I still keep it on every night.)

I'm sorry for turning up the volume when you started to play guitar, for giving you a hard time when you wanted to listen to Sinatra, and never letting you play video games.

I'm sorry for keeping you to myself and never wanting you to go fishing or anywhere without me.

I'm sorry for my suspicions, resentments, and the struggles I caused and created or didn't let go of.

I would tell you I forgive you for everything, too.

I would tell you thank you -for everything- for everything you did for us, for working so hard to provide for us, to give to us, to make life happen.

For making life possible.

I would tell you thank you for sticking with me when you should have run away and for coming back when you did run away.

Thank you for cooking and cleaning and grocery shopping, for running errands, and doing chores, for helping me with anything and everything.

For bringing me lunch or things I needed at work.

For buying me and the girls' pads, even though most guys think that's weird.

For pumping my gas - for meeting me across town just to pump my gas.

For never saying no and always trying to make everything work.

For helping me at work, at the theatre, at home.

For being an amazing husband and father.

For being an amazing lover, companion, partner, and friend.

For being an amazing person.

For giving me a chance all those years ago.

For fighting for me all those years ago.

For standing up to your parents all those years ago and for all the years that came.

For loving me when I didn't deserve it and for loving me way more than I ever deserved.

I would tell you thank you for being you.

I would tell you that I love you, that I miss you, that I want you, that I need you.

I would ask you to please come home. I would say please come home.

There Just Might Be

Sometimes I go into the bathroom and sit and cry. I go in there because it's where the kids can't hear me. Sometimes they catch me if they come in late at night. I try and wait until they are in bed, but sometimes I fail and they find me. They either walk away, ignore my state and ask their question anyways, or come and hug me for a moment. I usually wipe the tears away quickly and tend to their needs, pushing my pain away for the moment because they need me. What I really want is to just stand there and cry into your clothes. Your pants are still hanging from the door, grass stains on the knees from working in the yard those days before. Never got around to washing them that week. I can't find the strength to do it now. If I wash away the dirt, I might wash away the you. I stand there, leaning against the wall, buried in your pants. Sounds silly to say. Probably looks and seems pretty crazy. I stand there and I cry. And cry. And cry. There just might be more tears now than dirt.

Sometimes I hide in your closet, looking around at all that is you. Your shirts, your uniforms, equipment, gear, boxes of gun cleaning stuff and ammo. Pictures from the kids that you have tucked away, a picture of me, some other random boxes and such, a dresser never touched, everything as you left it. On top is your display box you got many years ago. I don't even remember when or where. It holds your pins, coins, old name plates, some other police memorabilia, some photos. I stand and look at all your things, signs of pride and honor. You were so proud of that badge. Wore it and represented it with such honor. A true peace officer, a true servant, one of the good ones. Your boots and a jacket lay on the floor, my wedding dress hangs in there too, because there was no room in my closet. I haven't opened the garment bag in years. I can't do it now either. Too painful. I should probably straighten up the closet some, but if I put things away, I might put away the you. Now your closet is just a museum. A hidden room that no one tends to. A hidden room where I cry. And cry. And cry. There just might be more tears than dust.

I stand at your counter. Your contact case sits just as you left it that night. Still open. Empty. Your razor by the sink. There are still a few beard trimmings left in the sink as well. I can't find the strength to rinse it out. If I rinse it out, I might rinse away the you. We've used some hair gel since you left, but we make sure to put the bottle right back to where it was. I hold your toothbrush next to my face. I know it's nuts. Weird. But it's one of the last things you touched that night. All your things are just as you left them that night. Your machete still lays there, too. Who in the world has a machete on their bathroom counter?! I look at it and remember the couple nights before when you gave it to me as a joke to cut a kiwi. I smile and let out a little chuckle remembering that moment. But then I just cry again knowing it's just a memory now. I really should throw away the old receipts and empty envelope, the trash and clutter, but I can't. I can't remove anything. My brain says if I put it away and you come back, you'll wonder where all your stuff went. I know that will never happen, but I just can't. I don't know when I will be able to. I can't even throw away the empty drink bottle by the bed, and I don't let anyone put anything on the bedside table either. Those are your places, your spots, your things. They are not mine to move, to throw out, to put away. I can't. So I just look at it all and I cry. And cry. And cry. There just might be more tears than clutter.

Not sure how after all these years, after all the love, all the life, but there just might be more tears than memories.

Our Star

—————————— * ——————————

Our star is back tonight.
I can see its glow so bright.
I wish I had a telescope to see you sitting there.
I wish I had a lasso to pull you back down here.
I wish I could build a rocket to send me up to you.
I wish I had a tree that could reach that high, too.
When I look up at our star, I feel you looking back.
With each glow and shine and sparkle, one more tear I lack.
If only stars could fall and drop right into reach,
I would hold my hands straight out all night and catch you as you leap.

—————————— * ——————————

Frozen

Someone described our home as frozen.
Like a coat of ice sealed the rooms.
Dust settling in the seams of the glaciers that hover
above and below,
capturing each item, belonging, each memory.
Everything frozen in time.
2:00am to be exact.
The moment time stopped.
The moment the ice began to spread.
The moment it all ended.
Frozen.

I hesitate to move things, change things, make things
new or different.
Fresh paint like you wanted, repairs that you couldn't
, a new pillow –
even though throw pillows serve no purpose –
a new candle as the one before no longer burns,
rearrange the photos to make room for your honors,
but don't change anything.
Keep it how it is.
How it was.
How you had it.
Let it be frozen.
Most importantly, don't take anything away.
We've already lost so much.
Lost everything.
Lost all hope, joy, and light.
We can't lose anything else.
Leave it in its place.
Frozen.

Make things look nice, live-able, welcoming - after all
I'm stuck here, alone for who knows how long.
But don't move Caleb's things.
Leave them in their place.
Frozen in time.
Everything frozen how it was.
Frozen.

Frozen as if we are waiting.
Waiting for you to return to unfreeze it.
Knowing you won't.
You can't.
Yet still hoping.
Still waiting.
Frozen.

Come back.
Come home.
Unfreeze this destitute of ice.
This burning ice.
Cold.
Dreary.
Sad.
Empty.
Lonely.
Frozen.

No heat remains.
No kindling left for fire.
Nothing to ignite.
Frozen.

But not just your belongings, your space, your things,
not just our home, our life, our memories, but our joy,
our energy, and light.
All frozen.

Eventually they will crack, shatter, dissolve.
Then what.

Then what.

120

A few weeks before Caleb was killed, I went through a bit of a "funk," as he called it. I felt a constant heaviness and uncertainty. Everything felt dreary and blah. Nothing seemed to bother me, yet everything bothered me. I shared my thoughts with Caleb and told him that I just had this feeling that things were "off." As always, he tried to reassure me that everything was ok, would be ok, and said, "There is no impending doom on the horizon." Well... he was wrong...

Impending Doom

I feel like I'm waiting for the dust to settle in an unsettled world.

I feel like I'm waiting for the fog to clear off the island of Newfoundland.

Like I'm waiting for the light to appear in the Mariana Trench.

Like I'm Noah, waiting for the rains to end with a hole in the ark and no canopy to provide cover.

I'm on the Titanic, watching slowly as the glacier pierces the steel
and the ocean begins to consume the ship with no rafts left to spare.

Standing in the heart of Pompei as the lava of Vesuvius rushes in and no higher ground in sight.

Waiting.

Fearfully waiting.

No safety.

No refuge.

No comfort.

No answers.

No where to go.

Nowhere to find help.

Nowhere to run and hide.

Consumed by fears, worries, problems, concerns, pain.

You said there was "no impending doom on the horizon..."

You were wrong.

And now I am alone.

Waiting with no end in sight as doomsday repeats infinitely.

When That Day Comes

Will I walk through the gate and casually look from side to side, over others, wondering where you are and knowing I will find you eventually...

Will I run through in desperation, knowing I've waited too long for this moment with so much anxious excitement bursting not wanting to wait a moment longer...

Will you be standing there waiting for me, watching, knowing I'm arriving any moment, ready to grab me and pull me in for that long overdue reunion...

Will it be so long from now that you don't even recognize me and I'll have to come and try and find you and tell you who I am...

Will you show me around and take me to see all the others who have been there before us and introduce me to your new friends...

Will we be so lost in the moment of being together again that nothing else matters...

Will they give us a few moments to catch up and hold each other before sending us to other tasks and needs...

I don't know what that day will be like, but I know that I will hold strong and try with everything I've got to ensure that that day comes...

I don't know when that day will come, but I will hold onto our love and count down the days until that joyous and liberating moment finally occurs...

One more day without you is one more day closer to being with you again.

Save me a spot, baby. I can't wait to see you again when that day comes.

John 16:22

What We Really Need

Talking about police stuff,
Telling me about guns and such,
Making plans for college and life,
Not sure what to say,
I don't know much about those things,
Her dad is what she really needs.

Accomplishments at school,
Preparing for senior year,
Becoming a beautiful young woman,
Not sure what to say,
I fight back tears as we talk,
Her dad is what she really needs.

Asking about girls,
Struggling in school,
Kids giving him a hard time,
Not sure what to say,
Always say the wrong thing,
His dad is what he needs.

Wanting to try new things,
Getting better at playing instruments,
Always in the kitchen like her dad,
Not sure what to say,
I can't help with those sort of things,
Her dad is what she needs.

Everything.
All of the above.
Life.
Love.
Family.
Her husband is what she needs.

Caleb is what we really need.

The Storm

I used to hate stormy days.
Dreary, cloudy, lonely, blistery days.
Gray and drab, depressing.
Everything gets drenched, muddy, sloppy.
Cold and wet, mucking about.
Loud, blooming, frightening.
Keeping you up at night.
Trapping you inside.
Storms bring destruction and despair.
Broken lands, floods, fear.
I used to hate stormy days.

But now,
I look outside and I see the beauty of nature.
I feel surrounded by your spirit with each moment the storm passes through.
The raindrops are the tears from heaven pouring down - cold, gentle tears that quickly become a flood racing down from the sky, rushing to meet me as if each drop is filled with your love.
Falling upon my face, fueled by your touch.
Drowning me in your grasp.
I feel your hands slowly reaching in as the rain puddles around my feet.
I hear your voice in the wind as it wraps around me.
The trees wave about as if you are dancing through the leaves, running to pull me to you.
I feel you hold me as the world trembles beneath the thunderous cries from above.
I look at the sky and with each flash and burst of fire beaming thru the clouds,
I see the glow from your smile, the oceanic sparkle from your eyes.
I hear the boisterous joy from your laugh with each rumble.
I stand outside as the world slows down, runs for safety, finding cover.
I stay outside for the storm is my refuge.
You are within the storm, and I recognize the peace that overcomes me.
I know the renewed life that is promised after the storm.
I know the you that lives on in me.

So, I no longer hate stormy days.
I welcome the clouds, the rain, the lightning blasting overhead, the thunder roaring all around as the storm pierces through the sky and meets the earth.
For in those moments - we are connected again - we are the storm.

The Bed

The bed is really big without you.
The wall is so far away - it's like the ocean - infinite, unending horizon.
It's cold and it's lonely.
It's weird because I slept alone in that bed for so many nights when you worked nights;
I hated it, but it didn't feel like this.
I still expect to wake up and see you sneaking in,
knowing you'll be climbing into bed soon.
I keep your side of the bed empty...just in case - I guess.
Your pillow, your fan, your slippers, your bedside table...just in case - I guess.
I make the bed every day - like you liked it.
You're right...it is more relaxing to get into a nicely made bed.
It takes me several minutes though.
I have to go from side to side, back and forth.
You could do it in one quick swoop.
I miss your "orangutang arms."
I miss having you beside me.
I still reach over to snuggle with you.
I put my hand on your chest, nose to nose, steal a little kiss.
Sometimes I think I hear you snoring.
I push you and tell you to knock it off.
This time though, the snoring stops.
It's quiet.
Silent.

The bed is so big without you.

Scars

I have a scar on my forehead.
Right in the middle.
It's just a little, tiny mark.
You can't really see it, but you can feel the slight indention in my skin.
It's been there since I was itty bitty...
too young to remember it happening.
I only know the story.
It has faded with time, but it's still there and I guess it will always be.

I have one above my right eye as well.
Just above my brow.
It's a little mark, too.
You can see it if you look close enough.
I can feel it every time I wipe away tears or sweat.

Sometimes I just touch it to see if it's still there.
We called it my "Harry Potter scar."
It's only a few years old.
I remember it happening.
Very well.
It's funny to talk about now.
You felt so bad for me.
I can still see the look of horror in your eyes.
I can still hear your voice, "Oh my gosh, baby, I'm so sorry."
I laugh every time I think about it.

I have other scars about - from scratches and old wounds.
Some scars you can see.
Some you can't.
Some you can feel.
Some are buried deep in the skin and don't have a mark.

I have a really big scar buried deep in my heart.
Deep in my soul.
The one left behind from the worst break of all, the biggest wound, the most horrid injury.
This scar you can't always see.
But I can feel it.
I don't want this scar.
I can never forget it and I can't laugh about it.
It will never go away.
I guess it might fade a little with time like the others.
But it will always be there.
I wish I didn't have this scar.

Midnight Thoughts, Midnight Tears

I am sad tonight. Sad for what our country has come to. The hate. The fear. The divide. Sad for people who have to defend themselves because of the color of their skin - and it goes both ways - it goes all ways!!! Sad for eggshells we have to walk on to not offend someone. I'm sad for police officers who have to live in fear and families who won't see their loved ones, their heroes. Sad for wives and husbands who will get a knock on their door in the middle of the night or tomorrow or the next day. Sad for sons who won't have their dad to play basketball with. Sad for daughters who won't have dads to walk them down the aisle. Sad for children who won't have their moms to argue with as teens, or hugs and kisses. Sad that my kids worry someone will break our windows because we have police stickers on our car. Sad that they are afraid people will hurt them because we support police. Sad that people say hurtful, hateful, disgusting things because their dad was a cop. Sad that I can't ease their pain. Sad that I can't do the one thing I am supposed to do and protect my children. Sad that some days I'm so sad I can't be a good mom. Sad that I have to pretend everything is ok. I'm sad that we can't have opinions without arguments and hateful and judgmental comments. Sad that expressing our feelings is considered complaining and being negative. Sad that people choose violence. Sad that every day there is another story on the news. Another way to cause division and hate and fear and chaos. Sad that Caleb's friends are out there tonight and that the number one officer who would have checked by on them is gone. Sad that my kids' father is gone. Sad that my husband is gone. Sad that my best friend is gone. Tonight I'm sad. I'm sad for me. I'm sad for my kids. I'm sad for our country. Tonight. I am sad.

A Mask of Many Faces

I get out of bed and put on mask number one - the morning face.
Get kids up and off to school, feed animals, housework, phone calls, emails, paperwork, forms,
keep it together, keep things going, get things taken care of, figure it out.
I leave the house.

Mask number two - the afternoon face.
Run errands, pay bills, grocery store, bank, various places, lunch meetings,
keep it together, keep things going, get things taken care of, figure it out.
I come back home.

Mask number three - the evening face.
Kids come home, help with homework, studying, chores, cook dinner, kids' sporting events, games,
practices, and activities, see people, family members,
keep it together, keep things going, get things taken care of, figure it out.

Mask number four - the night face.
The only face that's real.
The only face that's truly mine.

No mask at all.

Alone in bed, up half the night, tears, missing him, crying for him, quietly so the kids don't
hear, wishing there was someone I could call, someone still awake, someone who
understands, someone who can talk me out of this,
make the tears stop, someone who can bring him back.

No one.

So I put mask number one back on, wait for the alarm to go off, get out of bed
keep it together, keep things going, get things taken care of, figure it out,
and start all over again.

Auto Pilot

I am no longer living.

I merely exist within a weak shell of what I once was.

My joy and life and promise is gone,

so my breath and my beat and my mind are no more.

I exist as I move and continue life,

but I am no longer living.

I countdown the days and hope they lessen.

I hope for the clock to tick faster,

for the earth to make its rounds more quickly.

I hope for a push in time,

a blast forth,

for the sands to drop more heavily in the hourglass of life.

I walk through the world empty and void,

on auto pilot,

a robot.

I move through and accomplish life's tasks each day,

but I am no longer living.

My light went out as you gasped and let your last breath into the world.

Now I merely exist as I wait for the last of mine.

"When someone was so present and so large in your life...it's only natural that you can't comprehend their absence."

You think they are still around, may hear their voice or see their face -
it doesn't feel real, and you think they are out there some place.

Some say it's denial or not processing the grief,
but you just can't fathom they are gone - it's too hard to believe.

Your life is no longer the way it was before;
you no longer think, or feel, or even move the same way anymore.

You can't imagine having to go on without the light of your life,
and all you feel is agony, pain, and strife.

Your days become long, and the nights have no end,
and you fear your broken heart will just never mend.

The pain of the loneliness threatens your will,
and everything you do is a battle uphill.

Your home has a void and a darkness that fills each room;
it's constricting and breathless like being in a tomb.

An everlasting somber and doleful aura follows you each day,
and there's nothing you can do to get the agony to go away.

You have memories, pictures, and videos too,
but you just want your loved one back - nothing else will do.

The absence is overwhelming, and the emptiness is looming,
and you no longer want to live some days as breathing is too consuming.

Your world is upside down and every which way,
and your joy and strength slowly decay.

Not everyone truly understands or can really help you thru,
but you do the best you can and try and make do.

An occasional smile here and there or a day that passes by without too many tears,
and eventually you push forward as the days without your love turn into years.

Time goes on and there's nothing you can do,
so you just go one day at a time and hope your love is up there waiting for you.

That small fragment of hope is all that you hold,
until you are reunited again and can feel your love once more on those streets of gold.

Imagining that day is what sometimes helps you breathe,
as you are constantly knocked down by the waves of grief.

Just close your eyes and see your love's face,
listen to their voice, and feel their embrace;
imagine that day and even play out what you will say,
then take a deep breath and continue to face the day.

Little Pieces of You

She wiped off your counter and cleaned out your sink.
I told her to just leave your side alone,
but I guess she forgot or didn't understand.
Now all the little bits of you that were still there are
now gone.
Wiped away.
Washed out.
Gone.
Down the drain.
No more.
Your beard trimmings and prints.
The residue of shaving cream.
Little pieces of you.
Gone.
She moved things around.
I tried desperately to put them back.
Back to their exact location.
The very spot where you left them.
I couldn't remember exactly where some things went.
The precise angle and such.
You would think I would know.
I've stared at that counter for almost a year now.
Frozen in time.
Desperately longing for your return.
Everything where you had them.
Even the empty envelope, old receipt, crumbled bag,
paperwork, containers that should have been thrown
away.
Contact solution now expired.
Empty case dried up with no contents remaining.
Medication no longer needed.
Everything in the spot where you placed it.
Where your hands touched.
Where your prints were.
Where you were.
She moved things around and now the pieces of you
that were in those spots are gone.
Moved.

Repositioned.
Disrupted.
Little pieces of you.
Gone.
She tried to throw some things away,
but I noticed and dug them out of the trash bag.
Rescued them.
Replaced them.
Empty shampoo bottle, body wash, facial scrub.
Your shampoo.
Your bodywash.
Your facial scrub.
I couldn't find the bottle top though.
So now there is an empty spot where it was.
An empty spot on the counter.
An empty sink.
Empty spots everywhere where I knew you were.
Not just in the bathroom but all over our home.
Empty spots where you once were.
The bed.
The couch.
The chair.
Outside.
Inside.
In the car.
Spots where you were.
Where pieces of you were.
But now they are empty, and I can't refill them.
Some things I can't dig out and rescue.
I can't replace them.
Empty spots where pieces of you were.
Forever empty.
Little pieces of you.
Gone.
Little pieces of you.
Gone.
There are only so many pieces...

Storms

Most people hate storms.
Most people worry and fear storms.
Storms bring damage, pain, chaos.
Most people hate storms.
Storms break order.
Storms disrupt the day, destroy nature, damage life.
Storms are tragic.
They start slowly.
Skies darken.
Winds set in.
The clouds begin to cry.
They build.
They erupt.
The trees are shaken.
Leaves ripped about.
Warnings on tv, phones, social media.
Stay inside.
Stay off the roads.
Thunder screaming.
Lightning flaming.
Floods.
Damaging winds.
Hail.
Tornadoes.
Dark.
Loud.
Frightening.
Danger.
Tragic.
Most people hate storms.

But I understand the storm.
The storm speaks to me.
We connect.
The darkness.
The cries.
Screaming in my heart.
The fire in my empty soul.
Damage.
Destruction.
The whirlwind of change.
Of fear and pain.
Tragedy of death.
Loss.
Emptiness.
The storm rages through the skies and thru my veins.
I am the storm.
The storm ends and with each storm comes a new day.
Life keeps going.
The mess that's left behind gets cleaned up.
Things put back, replaced, rebuilt.
The storm ends and life re-begins.
The storm ends and life is forced to go back to how it was.
Everyone keeps moving as if nothing ever happened.
Everyone eventually goes back to normal.
Everyone pretends like it's all okay.
There is no choice.
No other option.

The storm ends but life is forced to keep going.
The storm ends –
But -
The storm returns.
There is no real end.

Contradictories

I'm alive but I'm not living.
Or maybe I'm living but no longer alive.
I can breathe, yet I gasp for air.
My heart beats even though it is shattered, broken, and in pieces.
Or maybe it no longer even exists.
I feel my pulse.
I hear the pulsating rhythms, but I don't even know if my heart still works.
A heart is meant for more than just moving blood.
A heart is meant to take in love, keep love, hold love...my love is gone.
Do I even need my heart anymore?
I can touch things even though it hurts too much to feel.
I can hear but everything is so quiet now.
Only silence.
I can see but I am constantly blinded by grief.
I walk.
I move.
But I am still.
I am stuck.
Frozen in despair.
I can speak, but I feel as if I have no one to talk to.
Not truly.
Not like what I need.
What I want.
Not the one I need.
The one I want.
I have my kids around me and a few others who check in from time to time.
But I am alone.
Lonely.
Solo parent.
One person who used to be a part of one.
Now left only half.

My other half is gone.
I am no longer legally married.
But I still wear my rings.
I still refer to my husband.
Think of my husband.
Want for my husband.
I still love my husband.
I will always love my husband.
But he is no longer considered my husband.
Why can't he be my husband.
I need my husband.
I have to check the box that says "widow."
I am called a widow.
But I am not a spider.
I am not a creature, but I no longer feel human so what am I anymore?
I exist but I don't live.
I only take up space.
But only half the space because all the other parts are empty.
Empty sink.
Empty bed.
Empty chair.
Empty but full of memories.
Full of his existence but not his presence.
Closet full of clothes that will never be worn.
Counter covered in belongings that no one uses.
A phone, a wallet, shoes.
Things that are his, but he is not here to have them.
If something exists but is never used again, does it really exist?
Do I really exist?
I am living but not alive.
Or maybe I am alive but not living.

Missing

You are missing so many things.
Missing everything.

The kids growing older.
Firsts.
Lasts.
Milestones.
Things Dads should be there for.

You missed Annie's graduation - both high school and military. You missed her college day and you'll miss moving her in and all of that.

You'll miss all their graduations and celebrations.

You missed the band concert, dance performances, and all Mark's football, basketball, and baseball games. He almost didn't even play because you were going to miss all the games. He doesn't want to play anymore at all.

You missed all Lizzie's soccer games, and she said she doesn't want to play anymore either. She wants to focus on theatre and band, but you are going to miss that too.

You missed Rosalan dancing this year and will miss her being an officer next year.
You missed out on so many things she accomplished this year.

You'll miss all their weddings and being a grandfather. I know you would have been such a good "Pops." You were such a good dad and uncle.

You are missing and missed and missing out on being a Dad.

You're missing everything.

Possessed

Sometimes I feel like I'm possessed.

Like something has taken over me and is controlling my every move.

I can't think for myself or do things for myself.

I have these rituals that I have to take upon and even when I stop and try to do something or not do something,

I can't.

I can't function or manage or think or decide or do the obvious.

I just move through space and time.

Move through each day but with no effort or thought.

It's like I am possessed.

Possessed - taken over, controlled, manifested, dominated.

Possessed.

But not in the evil, demonic sense of the word.

I am possessed by loss.

Possessed by grief.

By guilt and regret.

Possessed by desperation.

Desperate to remember.

To hold on to any and every little reminder, moment, memory.

Desperate to connect.

Desperate to find messages and signs.

Desperate to find meaning and purpose.

Possessed by emotions.

Breathless, pounding, aching possession.

I am possessed.

When will I be me again?

When will I be released?

Returned?

Freed?

When? How?

Is there even a way?

A Quiet Place

My quiet place isn't where there is tranquility and peace.
It's not where my soul can find joy or ease.
My quiet place is more like the movie.
Full of silence amidst a fearful journey.
My quiet place is filled with pain,
fear, turmoil, and torturous terrain.
No hope in sight.
Necessity fuels the fight.

The Waves of Grief

Some say grief comes in stages you pass through, sometimes repeat or loop.
Some say grief is like a hill or a mountain you climb up and down again.
Some describe it like being on a roller coaster - dipping, diving, speeding, and jostling.
I say grief is like the waves.

As I stood on the beach today, I watched the waves form and flow and form again.
I watched people interact with the waves and I watched the waves rush into the shore.
I watched the ebb and flow as the waves came in slowly, sometimes barely, and sometimes with force.
Some just at my feet, others at a distance, and many fading away far off into the sky.
As I stood watching the waves, I wrote this poem:

Watching the Waves -
The waves come in slowly, sometimes steadily,
but many come quickly without warning.
They are constant and never ending.
For brief moments there is a calmness as if the waves have gone away.
But another comes about soon behind, and another, and another after that.
Often knocking you down and taking your breath away.
Sometimes you can jump them, run away from them, or handle the hit.
Though you are jarred and thrown off balance,
you can stay afoot, stand tall, and only waver a bit.
But just when you think you've won the battle against the ocean's beast,
another gust from the tide comes about and throws you under its crest.
You gasp for air, choking for a breath, kicking your feet around.
Desperately, you reach for the bottom, the top, wherever gives you back your grip.
You find your stance and look around.
You wipe away the tears of salt, find your breath once more, and prepare to walk away.
You may feel knocked down and defeated, but you know that as you turn from the roars,
you have taken another step towards regaining strength.
The steps are often few and far between as the distance from the waves and the sand are overwhelming,
but the steps are steps nonetheless.
You eventually learn how to turn away from the waves;
although they will always exist,
you learn how to avoid them and step aside and watch from a distance.
On some days, the ocean may float away with more tallies of wins on the board,
but you are keeping count as well, and your tallies will eventually add up.
You will never truly win the fight, but you will never be taken completely under.
Do not fear - day by day, sometimes only moment by moment, you overcome the waves.
It may take time but take on the waves.
Do not just stand still, watching the waves as they look for their next victim, allowing them to claim you yet again -
Face the day, live your life, and rush into the water.
Take the battle of the waves.

Empty Rocking Chair

We had it all planned out.
We knew what life would be like.
We were looking forward to the days.
Making memories and making life together.
Living our best days - together.
A future full of possibilities.
Growing old - together.
Our final days - together.
Taking care of each other.
Grey-haired, sitting on the front porch.
In matching rocking chairs, surrounded by our grandchildren.
But now...

Life is frozen.
Never moving forward.
Growing old.
Alone.
Without you.
Without us.
Sitting on the front porch by an empty rocking chair.

Hidden Tears

I wipe away hidden tears because I have things to do.
Can't just lay around and cry all day when the house is
falling apart and there is so much relying on you and
you alone.
I can't drive the kids around and attend all their
functions when I'm full of tears.
So, I have hidden tears instead.

Inside I am crying.
Crying with frustration.
Crying with loneliness, sorrow, guilt, and regret.
Crying with emptiness.
Crying with exhaustion.
Overwhelmed by all the things I have to do.
All the things I must do alone.
I am crying all the time.
You can't see it, but I am.

I wipe away hidden tears when people come around.
They either don't say anything and awkwardly ignore
the tears anyways, or I get that look, that hug that says,
"I don't know what to do so…", or I get a poor attempt
at saying something to make it better.
Nothing will make it better anyways.
So, I have hidden tears instead.
It's just easier that way - I guess.
Besides the kids don't like it when I cry.
It makes them uncomfortable.
They don't say that, but I can tell.
So, I have hidden tears when they are around.

The hidden tears are most heavy when the kids are
around…because you are not around to see them.
To love them.
To be in their life.
Only I am here.
And I'm not that great.
You should be here.
So, I have hidden tears when the kids are around.
Because you are not.

I walk outside to tend to animals, check the mail, take
the trash, or just to get away for a moment.
Usually the tears follow me.
I only get a few minutes, so I let them out quickly for I
know I must hide them again within moments.
And I can't just stand on the driveway and wail to the
neighbors.
So, I have hidden tears instead.

I have hidden tears even at night.
Someone might hear or walk in.
They might need me, and I can't be a mother when I'm
soaked in tears.
So, I have hidden tears instead.

Sometimes when I go into the restroom, I take a
moment at your sink or in your closet.
I let the tears come out there.
But still, it's only for just a moment because well, you
know - I have kids and stuff to do.
So, I let the tears out for just a moment.
I soak them up with your clothes.
I probably look ridiculous standing at the closet door,
burying my face in your jeans that still hang from the hook.
I still can't clean off the counter.
I think about it from time to time, but I become
paralyzed.
People say I will know when it is the right time.
So, I stand there and look at your things - I pick them up
ever so gently and place them precisely back again.
Your counter and clothes are drenched in my tears.

But, as usual, someone walks in and I have to have
hide the tears again.

It's been a year, two months, and one week -
Should I still have the need to cry?
Should I still have this many tears?
A part of me is missing.
My heart.
My mind.
My body.
My soul.
My everything.
I look whole but a part of me is missing.
You can't see it - it is hidden.

Hidden with the pain.
Hidden with the anger.
Hidden with all the fears and paranoia that haunt me
each day.
Hidden with all the broken dreams, goals, and hopes
for the future.
Hidden with the wishes that this would all end.
Hidden with the resentments, the past that torments
me because there isn't anything to be done to fix it
now, but yet it still exists.
Hidden with the tears.

Backfired

I didn't like it when people commented, posted, or sent me a message.
So now no one says anything at all.

I didn't like it when people stopped by or called to ask how I was doing.
So now no one says anything at all.

I didn't like it when people tried to understand or compare their pains –
attempting to make me feel better as if their cat or cousin's death is anything like what I deal with.
So now no one says anything at all.

I didn't like people trying to take over, tell me what to do, or just do it themselves to not bother me.
So now no one says anything at all.

I didn't like to talk on the phone or have people come over to visit or meet up for lunch and dinner.
So now no one says anything at all.

I still don't really like any of these things happening, but I didn't mean for everyone to just disappear.

I guess it backfired on me, huh...

Blue Widow

"Blue Widow."

Sounds like a superhero
but likeness I have zero.

I don't have a cape to help me soar through the troubles that abound.
I don't hold a shield to protect me from the dangers around.

No armor I wear, no logo or sign;
I can't see through walls, and I can't change the time.

No special powers - no super strength or lightning speed,
no city calls from building top lights do I heed.

All I have is a hole in my heart and signs of weary on my face,
tears in my eyes, and forever an empty space.

"Widow" I'm now titled, like a creature of the night,
and "Blue" for the symbol of peace he did fight.

He was the hero - the one to whom a powerful name should employ,
yet it is I that must carry this designation that strips me of joy.

I hate this name, this new identity,
and all the pain connected to this responsibility.

But as a Blue Widow I also hold overwhelming pride,
for my husband was a hero and for his community he died.

Keeping us safe from the evils that prey,
willing to run into danger and step in harm's way.

My husband, my hero, forever my love,
and now my guardian angel still keeping watch – from above.

Hidden Landmines

I avoid the grocery store - curbside or delivery is what I must do.
Too many people and families reminding me of what I no longer have.
Hidden landmines.

Restaurants are hard - I know what you would have ordered.
I see couples on dates, laughing, smiling, holding hands.
Hidden landmines.

Dads with their kids.
Husbands and wives.
Elderly couples - together for so long.
Hidden landmines.

Driving around town is no easy task.
We liked to go there…we went there one time…
we never got to go there…
Hidden landmines.

Stories in the news.
Another officer. Another officer. Another officer.
Especially when they say "fortunately the officer survived…"
Hidden landmines.

Nowhere is safe.
Everywhere I look ignites pain, fears, anger, and tears.
Hidden landmines.

New things around the house - painted the walls, the furniture you ordered finally arrived, added a few
 things here and there, moved things around, on every wall are pictures of you, and the living room is full of memorial plaques, décor, and such.
Hidden landmines.

Repairs and projects left undone, plans and things we intended to do.Hidden landmines.

The flowerbeds are changed - I didn't do a good job at keeping everything you had planted. I'm sorry.
The yard is a mess - I keep trying to find help.
So many things I need to do, get fixed, take care of.
Hidden landmines.

The porch should be welcoming, yet it too holds silent ammunition.
The wreath on the door is a reminder of the day, along with the blue bow and sign that leads the way.
Even the rocking chair sitting empty on your side.
Hidden landmines.

The office, the kitchen, the counters, the table - every room holds signs of your life,
yet no signs of your life fill the room.
Hidden landmines.

Movies, songs, tv shows.
Sights, sounds, smells.
Sayings, quotes, jokes.
Sometimes even when I see someone do something a certain way.
Hidden landmines.

No way to avoid them.
They are everywhere.
No way to detect them.
They often come out of nowhere.
They are everywhere.
Hidden landmines.

Everywhere.
Everywhere where you should be.
Hidden landmines

Not Another Poem

No, it's not another poem.
It's not in rhyme or rhythm of any sort.
It's not really even in prose.
It's not another poem.
It's just a statement.
A powerful one.
One that controls my every thought.
My every move determined by one statement consisting of four words.
One statement of my life forevermore.
It's not another poem.
It's just the truth.
The facts.
Reality.
My new life.
My every day.
It's not another poem.
It's just this:

I need my husband.

Eeny, Meeny, Miny, Mo

Life is a game of
      Eeny, Meeny, Miny, Mo.

Who will get ridiculously good looks, an amazing body, genius abilities or talents....
      Eeny, Meeny, Miny, Mo.

Who will have things handed to them, or not have to work hard in life to earn riches, or have wealth or special opportunities and such...
      Eeny, Meeny, Miny, Mo.

Who will be born into wealth or fame or have opportunities come to them through life to lead them this way...
      Eeny, Meeny, Miny, Mo.

Who will have a plethora of family and close friends to be with them all throughout their life...
      Eeny, Meeny, Miny, Mo.

Who will have physical or mental health and well-being and safety for all throughout their life...
      Eeny, Meeny, Miny, Mo.

Who will get healing, recover from injury, get better, make it out ok, survive, be cured...
      Eeny, Meeny, Miny, Mo.

Who will receive miracles and if harm comes their way they will be rescued or spared and get to live another day...
      Eeny, Meeny, Miny, Mo.

Who will get to live a long, happy, love-filled life with their one and only...
      Eeny, Meeny, Miny, Mo.

      Eeny, Meeny, Miny, Mo...

      ...and you are not it.

Fraud

Fraud.

Fake, phony, imposter.

Pretending, impersonating, lies.

> Smile.

> Look ok.

> Get stuff done.

> Keep it together.

> Visit, talk on the phone, go places.

> Friends for lunch, an occasional night out, people over.

> Laugh.

> Be happy.

Fraud.

Fake, phony, imposter.

Pretending, impersonating, lies.

Wish We Would Have Had More

An evening alone, date nights, weekend getaways - few and far between.
Hurts when I see other couples on date nights and vacations together.

Wish we would have had more.

Mainly ours were only dinners - a couple fancy ones, mostly just somewhere close in town - quite a few movie theaters and some movies cuddling together on the couch, Phantom at the theatre, Romeo and Juliet at the ballet, concerts at the fair and rodeo, a few holiday parties, a night out in Galveston a few times, a weekend in San Antonio a couple times, a night out once in Austin, won a trip to Nashville one time which was pretty awesome, went on a cruise together twice which was really awesome.

Wish we would have had more.

Seems like a lot of time together, sounds like a lot of memories but not near enough for nearly twenty years together.

Wish we would have had more.

Demanding work schedules, conflicting nights off, kids busy with activities and events, no babysitter, tired from work, long drives to somewhere decent, late nights and early mornings don't mix, wish he liked to dance - I really liked going dancing but didn't like going to bars. Not many options. Not a lot of extra money. Not enough extra time.

Wish we would have had more.

That last Tuesday's scheduled date night got ruined... Wednesday's date night redo was just watching a movie after the kids went to bed and spending time together in our room. But it was our last night together.

Wish we would have had more.

Nothing fancy. No money spent. No stress of finding an outfit, babysitter. No scheduling issues. No problems or excuses. Not really even a date night. Not really anything amazing. Just a movie in our room and a few hours alone.

Wish we would have had more.

It was almost perfect.
Our last night together.

Wish we would have had more.

Before & After

<table>
<tr><td>

Before:

Organized (Overly)

Focused

On top of things

Sharp

Together

Complete

Efficient

Driven

Smart

Confident

Happy

Loved

Living

</td><td>

After:

Jumbled

Distracted

Forgetful

Lost

Broken

Empty

Crazed

Distant

Inadequate

Anxious

Miserable

Lonely

Lifeless

</td></tr>
</table>

We Had Plans

We had plans for the coming days.
We were going to go grocery shopping when you woke up.
Get all the food for Annie's party.
Do some last-minute things around the house.
Get ready for graduation.
Celebrate our little girl.
Be together to see our little girl walk across that stage.
We had plans to go to dinner afterwards.
Probably Texas Roadhouse.
We had plans to get up the next day and get everything set up for the party.
We had plans to celebrate with our family and friends.

We had plans for your birthday the next week.
You said we didn't need to go out to eat and do anything special, so we had plans to just do something at home instead.

We had plans for the summer.
Summer camps at the new theatre, maybe try and go to the lake together again, maybe as a family this time, do all we could as a family before Annie left for boot camp and moved to college.

We had plans for stuff at work.
We had plans for the schedule to sort out and get back in order once your move to traffic enforcement happened.

We had plans for the years to come.
We had plans for some trips.

We had big plans for our 20th Anniversary. Vow renewal. Ceremony the way we want without conditions from others who were involved the first time. A big party. A dance. A fresh start.

We had plans for when the kids were all moved out.
We had plans to spend more time together, just the two of us.

We had plans for retirement.
We had plans to move to the mountains, run a bed and breakfast.

We had plans for our future.
We had plans to grow old together.

We had plans.
All those plans were ruined.
This was not the plan.
Sometimes plans change.
But this –
THIS IS NOT WHAT WE PLANNED!

Becoming Normal

Sometimes I feel like you're not really gone, sometimes I forget that you're gone, and sometimes it feels as if you never even existed.

It feels like my old life was so long ago, like a distant memory, a different life, in a different time.

I get through the day sometimes as if nothing has changed - even though everything has changed.

Sometimes I sit and cry and can barely catch my breath from the pain, and other times I can't even find anymore tears.

It's those moments that hurt the most.

> I hate that this life is becoming normal.

I tend to the kids, manage the house, the bills, try my best to get things taken care of, keep up with tasks, and chores, and things to do, and sometimes it just all gets taken care of without a second thought - almost as it this is how it's always been.

Of course, other times I can barely get out of bed, I can barely function, I can't focus, I can't get going, I can't even face the world.

Somedays I can't remember what needs to be done, and most days I don't even know how to do things.

And then there are days when I figure it out.

> I hate that this life is becoming normal.

In the moments of this new normal, I feel guilt.

I feel like I'm betraying you, dishonoring you.

I'm afraid you are looking down and thinking we've forgotten you, moved forward, moved on.

I'm afraid your presence will fade and disappear.

Sometimes I wonder if I'd even notice - sometimes I fear I won't.

> I hate that this life is becoming normal.

I'm afraid you'll stop visiting and being around.

If you don't think we need you, you won't be here anymore.

But then the overwhelming,

grief-ridden feeling that you're not really gone takes over and I think you are out there, somewhere, and will call or come home.

I cry out for you. Beg for you to come back.

Scream even.

Sometimes I look at your pictures, your belongings, even your name, and I wonder where you are and what's taking you so long to come home.

Then I remember.

I cry, I hurt, I hope it will all end soon, and then I eventually dry my eyes, and go to sleep, get back on task, continue the conversation and keep going.

> I hate that this life is becoming normal.

It's like I'm stuck on repeat, looped, frozen in time and will never move forward.

Truthfully, I don't want to move forward.

Moving forward means I'm leaving you behind.

It means I've accepted this life.

It means this really is my new normal.

> I hate that this life is becoming normal.

I don't want this life.

I want you back.

I don't want to forget.

I don't want to be "ok" –

nothing about not having you is ok.

Yet, everything around me appears to be "ok."

And I am not ok with that.

> I hate that this life is becoming normal.

Couples

Couples at the store shopping together -
some look as if they are just starting life as one,
some have children and many years to see,
some are old and have so many stories to tell.

Couples at the restaurant –
date nights, smiling, laughing, holding hands, spending time together.

Couples at the park, at the post office, at the bank.

Couples at parties, at events, throughout town.

Sitting at the table, seeing the couples.
He puts his hand on her back, she brushes away the stray hair on his jacket.
Whispers and grins, sneaking a kiss, dancing, helping her with her chair,
getting her drink, holding hands.

Group photo –
all the couples...
and then me.

Sometimes I wish I had just stayed at home.

Growing Old

I wish I could grow old with you.
Wrinkles and crinkles and grey hair.
Well, most likely no hair for you.
Slow moving and telling the same stories over and over.
Well, you already started doing that!
Coffee with every meal and Denny's early morning dates.
Newspapers and bird watching.
I think that's what old people do.
Rocking chairs and his and hers recliners.
Falling asleep early and afternoon naps.
Grandkids and maybe even great grandkids.
Sitting in our laps.
Gigi and Pops.
That's what I think they would call us.
Holding hands and helping me up the stairs.
Bones creaking and Epson baths.
Talking about "the good ole' days" and griping about "kids these days."
Sneaking sweet kisses.
Still just as much in love as we were way back then.
That was the plan...
It was a good plan...
Growing old with you.

Not in the Dictionary

Grief is silent...
yet deafeningly loud.

Grief is lonely...
yet overwhelmingly crowded.

Grief is invisible...yet blindingly apparent.

Grief happens suddenly...
yet lasts indefinitely.

Widow

I am not a creature hiding in the corners,
hunting in the dark,
luring in my prey.

I am not creeping through the trees,
catching those who cross my web,
devouring those who stay.

Yet, they still call me a widow.

I've been told in the eyes of the law, my vows no longer remain;
I am no longer united by the symbol of the ring or sanctity of their exchange.

I've been told I must choose the last box now -
the title that makes me cringe and strikes my heart like a dagger.

I still feel the love of that 6th day of April, all those years ago –
just the same as I did and always will.

I still feel the power in his and my name and why it exists.
I still long to hear Mrs. and state that I am.

Yet, they still call me a widow.

I do not want that title and all that comes with it.

Why must I feel the weight of the monstrous creature that it depicts.

Christmas Eve

Rooftops, windowpanes, and sidewalks, lined with Christmas lights.
Homes filled with giddiness and joy, awaiting what surprises and magic await.
Tables surrounded with families, sharing stories, memories, and laughter.
Gifts and treats, sounds of jubilee.
The season of hope, miracles, and love, celebrating the birth of our savior.
Faith abounds and the aura of life fills the air.

But for me - the lights are blinding, the magic nothing but a farce,
the table surrounded by deafening sounds of silence as the chair on the end sits empty,
hopelessness, unanswered prayers, and loneliness.
Faith weakens and life means nothing without you.

Loneliness

Loneliness is crippling.
Silent yet blaring.
Seeing others with friends and family and support.
Gatherings, parties, dates, photos, people coming over, getting together.
A few texts and check-ins but rarely an invite.
Longing for companions and inclusion.
Busy but empty.
What will my legacy be if I have no one to have it with?
Wishing for more than just being a mom.
Who am I if no longer his wife.
Lonely nights.
Lonely days.
In a few years the kids will all be moved out.
Will friends be there then?
At least now I have things I have to do.
What loneliness awaits me then if I already feel it now?

Puzzle Pieces

If we stand together and hold one another,
I meet just beneath your chin,
allowing you to rest your head upon mine as I lay my face upon your chest,
breathing you in.
Fitting together as one.

Or if I stand with you behind me,
I can lean back and fit just right so that your arms wrap around me
and neither has to bend or tilt.
Fitting together as one.

As we walk side by side,
our arms are at the exact length to hold arms without any effort.
Fitting together as one.

As we lay together,
our bodies fit just right,
my hips pulled back in the crevice of you,
our knees slightly forward,
and our souls unite with ecstasy.
Fitting together as one.

Each part of me fits precisely within your reach.
Within your grasp. Your step. Your touch.
I may have to tip toe just a bit to kiss you straight on,
but as our lips connect,
the rhythm of our hearts become one beat.
Fitting together as one.

Every curve, every strand, every fragment of life.
Fitting together as one.

Perfect puzzle pieces.

Say it Back

Sometimes I wouldn't say it back.
I'm sorry I was so stubborn.
Stupid.
Selfish.
Upset or angered.
Annoyed and bothered by nonsense.
Stupid.
Selfish.
Oh, how I wish I could hear those words again.
How I yearn to be able to say it back.

But sometimes I wouldn't say it back because I wanted to savor the sound
of hearing you say it to me.
I wanted to breathe in the words.
Let them ignite through my body and blaze through my soul.
I wanted to feel the passion that came with each letter,
fueling our bodies and commitment to one another.
I wanted to feel the power of each word,
lifting me through any moment of fear, weakness, or doubt.

Oh, how I wish I could hear those words again.

How I yearn to be able to say it back.

How I need to hear those words again.

How I need to be able to say it back.

I Know What It's Like

The weight of grief is like an endless beating from the waves of the ocean.

The darkness of a broken heart is like the vantablack of a night with no stars.

The silence of loneliness is like a vast galaxy with no existence.

Wanting to live but wanting so desperately for God to take you.

Hoping each day will be your last.

Crying out, "Take me now."

An end to the emptiness.

Wanting an end but not having the courage to do it yourself.

The fears of what comes with that hopelessness.

Holding onto what little faith you can muster and knowing if you end the pain,
the arms of your beloved won't be there to welcome you in.

And knowing what pain is left behind if you do end the pain.

Knowing the pain and not wanting to be the cause of more pain
but not wanting to endure the pain any longer
and not knowing how to end the pain without ending the pain.

The heaviness.

The beating of the waves.

The darkness.

The brokenness.

The silence.

Desperation.

Hope.

Emptiness.

Fear.

Hopelessness.

Faith.

Pain.

The Mirror

Some days I just stand here,
and I look at myself in the mirror;
I see the pain and the signs of sorrow,
and I can't even imagine facing tomorrow.

I look into my eyes, searching desperately for the me I used to be -
I know she's gone 'fore there can't be a me without a we.

The strength, the passion, the fight;
it all went away on that horrible night.

I haven't accepted this new me that I have become -
this me who lives in a world of darkness, void of the sun.

This me who is broken and incomplete -
who feels frozen and numb, with an endless day stuck on repeat.

The sun goes down and the moon comes out,
and the hours pass by and the sun continues its route,
so I know it's not a blackhole or a rip in space,
but I can't help but see that time has been warped as I look at this face.

I feel like it's stopped, yet it looks like it's elapsed years of wear in these troubled eyes;
I try to keep faith and search for some hope,
but I can't help but feel I've reached the end of my rope.

How can I keep going and force this worn-out soul?
How can I get up when I've fallen so low?

I look at my reflection through the words written on the glass;
I straighten my focus and take a step back,
and there in front of me is the poem you wrote for me;
"I Love You...I Believe in You" are the words that I see,
and as my face is covered yet again in tears,
I take a deep breath and try and look past the stress, the strain, and the fears.

I imagine you pulling me in close and wrapping me into your embrace,
and in that moment, some joy returns to my face.

The strength that I need is pulled from within,
and I shall press on for I know that I shall be with you again.

One day, some day, when my time is through,
but until that day comes, I will believe in me, too.

You Are Not There

I wake each morning and turn to look for you,
but yet again, you are not there.

Hoping for a miracle, a trip back in time, a do-over, a second chance,
but yet again, you are not there.

Perhaps I was stuck in a time warp, or a long-standing nightmare, maybe it's only been a cruel and confusing prank-
but yet again, you are not there.

I hear footsteps approaching in the early morning light –
you are home from work, tiptoeing in the room using your phone to guide the way so I'm not disturbed,
though I wake at the sound each time - I turn to look for you,
but yet again, you are not there.

My phone chimes at a late-night hour –
you are checking in, sending me an update or a message about a crazy call, calling to say good night and I love you –
I turn to look for you,
but yet again, you are not there.

I hear the opening credits from one of your silly shows –
I would've rolled my eyes and said turn that off, it's so stupid, but I let you watch it because then I hear your laugh -
the antics begin, so I turn to look for you,
but yet again, you are not there.

I see the glow from the computer screen bellowing under the door –
maybe you've been in there all this time, working on pictures or video,
you're taking a little break and reading an article, leaning back in the chair and turn around as I walk in -
but yet again, you are not there.

A song comes on the radio –
one of your favorites, one that reminds me of you, or the song from your alarm –
I turn to look for you,
but yet again, you are not there.

The restless bathroom counter, the unbothered closet, the quiet kitchen, the dust covered piano,
the untouched guitar, the lonely camera, the empty driveway –
every spot you touched,
I touch to look for you,
but yet again, you are not there.

The celebrations, milestones, and moments of our children's lives,
I turn to look for you,
but yet again, you are not there.

I wake each morning and turn to look for you,
but yet again, you are not there.

One Day at a Time

Maintaining composure gets tiring after awhile; it's exhausting always having to force a smile.
I'm filled with so much sorrow and nothing is fine, but all I can do is take it one day at a time.

Holding back the tears and moving through the day when all I want to do is just run away.
I'm filled with so much sorrow and nothing is fine, but all I can do is take it one day at a time.

Having to pretend like I'm strong and alright is a constant battle, a daily fight.
I'm filled with so much sorrow and nothing is fine, but all I can do is take it one day at a time.

I have so much to do and so much to face; life as a solo parent is a never ending race.
I'm filled with so much sorrow and nothing is fine, but all I can do is take it one day at a time.

I have to stay busy and wipe away the tears; I don't have time to worry or face all my fears.
I'm filled with so much sorrow and nothing is fine, but all I can do is take it one day at a time.

I must force myself to breathe and ignore the pain, but I am withering from the stress and the strain.
I'm filled with so much sorrow and nothing is fine, but all I can do is take it one day at a time.

Another Night

Another night, another empty bed,
another lonely date with just the memories in my head.

Another day, continuous hours of wicked waiting;
there's only so much one can take before your spirit starts fading.

Another moment of wishing you were here, longing for your touch,
screaming in silent disarray from missing you so much.

Another tear upon my face, another break within my heart,
another night, another day, another moment we're apart.

Another this, another that, another reminder you're not here;
another special day that you have missed, another empty chair.

#SavedYouASeat
John 16:22

I Guess

I guess by now we've started to adapt.

I guess that's what happens, and I guess that's ok.

We have to keep going and we have to move forward - but that doesn't mean we've moved on.

I guess we just get used to making things work and I guess we just get thru the days - but that doesn't mean we're ok.

I still long for your touch, and yearn for your voice, and ache for your presence.

I still think about telling you something, or ask you about something, or wonder what you will say or do.

I still look for you, listen for you, and talk to you - I even talk back for you and I guess that's ok.

Doing things we said we would do is hard to do, but we do it because I guess we have to.
I hate that we can because you are gone, and I hate that we do it because you are gone.

I guess we just make it work and we figure it out, and I guess that's ok because that's what you would do.
I guess the kids are doing ok, and I guess that's ok - but it doesn't mean it's ok that you're gone.

I'm not really ok, but I guess I have to be - or at least I try to be. I guess I seem to be at least.
I don't really know what ok really means. If I say we're ok, then it's like it's ok that you're gone and that's not ok.
I guess it's ok that we're ok, because that's what you would want us to be - but it doesn't mean it's ok.

I know one thing at least that is ok and that I don't just guess, and that's that I'll see you again someday.

Until then we just have to adapt. We have to keep going and move forward.
We have to make things work and get thru the days.
We have to make it work, and figure it out, and we have to try and be ok.
I'm not ok...but I guess I have to just seem ok.

Reality

Sometimes it feels as if it were all a dream, a story, a different era or time,
and then the reality of this pain sneaks back in and strangles me from the inside out.

I reach deep within to try and grasp memories, reminders, images from times together,
only to once again be attacked by the monster of grief.

I look through photos, videos, and treasures of our life,
but tears pour in and I weaken with regrets and guilt.

I think to call you, ask you a question, tell you about something,
thinking you are out there, lost and waiting to come home.

I forget. I remember.

I want to forget. I want to remember.

Forget the pain. Remember the joy.

Forget you left. Remember you're gone.

Wish it were not real.

Wish you were home.

A dream, a story, a different era or time.

The reality.

Missing You

I missed you today like I always do.
I missed you yesterday, and I'll miss you tomorrow, too.

I missed you at the day's end and all thru the lonely night,
and I missed you again with the silent morning light.

I missed you at dinner, seeing the empty chair, and at every holiday, special event,
and every gathering that you're not there.

I miss you every minute and every second that you're gone,
and I'll miss you every moment until my breath is done.

I miss you now and I'll miss you then,
and I'll miss you all the days until we meet again.

John 16:22

Don't Say

Don't say, "we lost you," because he can never be found again.

Don't say, "my late husband," because he'll never show up on time again.

Don't say, "he's passed, died, deceased...,"
and oh, how I hate, "he's gone home, in a better place, or it was his time."

It's pretty messed up if this is the way God tests us or tries to get us to reach out,
and there is no purpose, lesson, or reason for this tragedy.

The truth of the matter is - he was taken from us, ripped from life, robbed from time, killed.

It's not right. It's not fair. It's not how our life is supposed to be.

Nothing will make it better, so don't bother with the sentimental wastes.

Inspirational sayings, quotes, and scriptures don't help.

Therapy isn't a magic cure, talking about it won't make me feel better,
and time won't heal these wounds (or his).

Not Your Typical Fortune Cookie

"The fear you must feel having to face the future without the one you planned it with."
(A good family friend told me this one day. He was a constant comfort to me, checking in every few days or so.
He always knew the right things to say at the moments I needed to hear them.
I could write a second book full of just his emails and messages.)

———————————————

It's not until you can't say "I love you" anymore that you really
understand how much you mean it.
(I came up with this one...although I'm sure many people have felt this.)

———————————————

You don't "get" through grief and loss, you "go" thru it - every moment of every day.
(I came up with this one as well after someone told me they hope I can get through my loss and put it behind me.
I think we can all agree that was a dumb thing to tell me.)

———————————————

You don't deal with it either; instead, you have to force yourself to just do it
and try and re-survive – every moment of every day.
(My words as well – what's that saying, those who can't do, teach.)

———————————————

"Having to do all the parenting and housework and decision making
and everything on your own... with no expectation of change..."
(My best friend said this to me one day after her husband was out of town for several days.
All I have to say is, solo parenting and single parenting are two different things.)

———————————————

A boat cut loose from the dock with nothing to hold on to.
Drifting helplessly further and further.
(No real story behind this one, just something I thought of one day and felt it so deeply.)

———————————————

The greatest love bears the greatest grief.
(Saw this once and really felt it, too. Caleb and I had a cliché fairy tale love story, knowing each other since we were
kids, forming a relationship through high school, married right away...we were supposed to grow old together and
have a happy ever after. My grief is sometimes so overwhelming, I physically cannot fathom living anymore, but I
know it is because I loved so deeply, so greatly, and a part of me is missing.)

Tears and Time

What if the tears eventually stop?
They seem to be slower these days.
I know how to turn them off or keep them away it seems.

Or maybe my brain is just working overtime so I'm not sitting here crying nonstop.
Because if I could, I would.
I would just lay here and cry an endless pool of sorrow and loneliness.
A downpour of pain and torturous grief.
I would completely and utterly drown in my own tears.
I think I could literally do that if I allowed myself to.

But I don't have time to do that.
I have to turn them off and keep them away.
I have to shut it down.
Hold it back.
Tuck it away for when I can let it out.
Or when I really need to let it out.

Sometimes though, lately, it seems like the tears have slowed down.
The things I would just lose it over, I can handle.
I can choke it back.
It hurts to.
And it just plain hurts altogether.
But I can breathe and wipe my eyes and turn the thoughts off for a bit when I need to.

But the truth is….

It hurts to say that I can.
I hate that I can.
I don't want to feel like it's okay now.
I don't want to feel like it's normal now that you're gone.
I don't want to feel like I've gotten used to it.
I hate the pain, but I hate not having it either.
I can't have both.
But both are equally as painful.

Or maybe I'm just out of tears.
Maybe my emotions are so tired from being overloaded that they have just left my body.
Maybe it's not that I can handle it better.
Maybe my body just can't take it anymore and shuts itself off for me.
Maybe it's not me.

Or maybe it's just part of this horrific journey of grief.
Maybe the steps are true.
Maybe there is "acceptance" and maybe I'm there.
But what if I don't want to "accept" this.
How could anyone "accept" this pain.
This sorrow and loneliness.
How could anyone be ok without their love.
Their life.

Maybe it's all of the above.
Maybe that's just what happens after a while.
Maybe the cliche sayings are correct.
They say it gets easier with time, better, different….

What if one day the tears eventually stop?
What if they never do?

Do I have the choice between the two?

Never Again

I thought I was just sending you off to work.
Just another normal day.
A quick kiss goodbye.
A talk to you later.

But there will never again be a normal day.
There will never be a longer kiss hello.
We will never talk later.

Saved You a Seat

We saved you a seat at dinner tonight;
all the family was gathered - it was a beautiful sight.

We saved you a seat at the birthday and holiday celebrations,
Rosalan's dances, Lizzie's concerts and shows, Mark's games, all their graduations.

We saved you a seat on the front row of Annie's wedding;
you not being there was beyond upsetting.

You were supposed to walk her down the aisle and Lizzie and Rosalan when their day arrives;
you're supposed to help Mark with his tie and spend time with him - just the guys.

He needs a man to lead him through life,
teach him how to be a dad and be good to his wife.

All our grandkids need their Pops to play with them outside –
you were supposed to count while they go hide.

We were supposed to retire, move to the mountains, and open a B&B –
grow old together with a love so deep.

You won't be here for any of these things;
all we have now is your empty saved seat.

Alone

Lying alone,
pictures and videos on my phone are all that gets me through the nights.

Sitting alone,
thoughts and memories in my mind are how I move through the days.

Each night.
Each day.

Every night.
Every day.

Alone.

Even in a crowded room.
Even with people around.
Alone is how I feel.

Time Moves Forward but Some Things Stand Still

As time moves forward and life grows around the wound,
it's not that I'm ok now.

How could I ever be?

It's not that I've gotten used to you being gone,
I still expect you to come home at times.

It's not that things are better now,
it's just that life keeps on despite.

It's not that it doesn't hurt anymore,
I've just gotten numb to the pain.

I don't cry as much or as often anymore,
I've learned how to turn it off when I have to.

I don't beg for you to come home anymore,
I realize how useless those screams are.

I still talk to you like you are here,
I still reach out and imagine you are here.

I still hold on to the blueprint of your body, the feeling of being in your arms,
your eyes, your smile, your touch, your voice.

I still think what it would be like if you were here –
what we would be doing, what you would say, what you would think of things, and such.

As time moves forward,
some things stand still –

I still wish you were… instead of was.
I always, always will…

Inosculation

"Inosculation is the phenomena of tree roots growing around something.
The object, once the tree has enveloped, is called an inclusion."

I was looking at pictures of trees that had grown around various items that were placed too closely to the tree in its youth or items that had been unattended for too long - items such as old bikes, cars, fences, signs, and such; there were even some photos of parts of a house. The trees had basically engulfed the item and the bark molded around the shape of the obstacle. The branches were rearranged and the trunks deformed, but surprisingly the trees continued to grow, even blossom in spite of the invasion. The trees didn't all look like a normal tree in many ways, yet they all seemed to function as though everything was ok. You couldn't see the insides to see if the rings were destroyed or if any internal damage was done to the trunk or roots, but from the outside, it looked like the tree had adapted and was just fine - except for the giant protrusion of course.

I feel like those trees. The obstacles are the destructive pain of losing Caleb that has engorged my spirit, just like the tire sticking out of one side, the fence post stabbing through at one end. I often show signs of his absence, but in general, from the outside, I guess you could say I look ok - normal, in some ways. I continue to live and manage through the days. Just like the trees have continued to grow with the passing of time, life continues to grow around me and move forward with the tides. The days press on with no regards to the estranged nights. I smile when there is reason for joy, even in the crushing pain of knowing Caleb is not a part of it. I seem ok, but you don't see the mess within.

As so, the trees look ok, but you don't see where the green bark is defaced, you don't see where the roots have been disjointed, you don't see where the rings have been mangled. It looks like the tree is adapting as it reforms around the impairment, but the interior is most definitely damaged. How could it not be. You don't hear its cries and because of this, you assume it has healed; you praise the tree for staying strong and commend it for pushing through. This is its life now. Day end and day out. A broken marvel.

There's nothing the tree can do at this point. Through time, perhaps the item will loosen from the grasp of the wood; it may even fall out completely if nature or human assist, but there will forever be signs of the intrusion. There will forever be a mark of the impingement. The tree may press on - upward and outward. It may bring forth fruits and carry on as a somewhat productive member of the forest…even with the trespassers. The tree may remain in tact, yet no amount of time will ever truly repair the affliction.

Balance

One foot carefully placed in front of the other,
teetering high above the ground,
slowly stepping with arms outward,
eyes focused on only the step ahead,
for looking too far in front throws off my balance and I risk falling.
Stacked upon my shoulders and stuffed in bags I struggle to grasp in each hand
are the mass of the day's demands.

Every question, every need, every want and request, every decision, every choice, every task, chore, responsibility,
daily labor, all the moments of life and commands of the day
weighing upon me as I struggle to slide forward along the beam.

Balancing the busy days with the emptiness of the nights.

Balancing the blade of loneliness with the gut-wrenching fear of the thought of replacement.

Balancing the memories with the moments,
the joy with regret,
the sorrow with bliss.

Life pulls me to the left and I wobble, almost dropping one of the weights.

I recorrect and lean back to the right, hoping to steady my stance,
but with no one to grab,
no one to lean on for support,
no one to catch me and assist,
I fall.

I lay still,
beaten, bruised, buried.

I can't be expected to carry this burden on my own through the obstacles and hurdles
with no warning,
no preparation,
no way to ready myself.

I can't stay on the narrow beam with all this weight pulling me from one side to the other,
pulling me down.

I can't balance it all on my own and still be expected to step forward,
to keep moving,
to make it to the end.

I can't.

I can't balance.

Thoughts...Wishes

Sometimes I think, why couldn't it have been one of the other officers on the scene...

One of them had no kids, she wasn't married, she was young. Yes, she had a future, but I can't help but focus on the fact that she didn't have a present...

What about the other officer?

He was young too. He was married and had a little boy, but his boy was little - too little to really understand. Too little to really know the pain. Too little to really remember. I can't help but think it would've been a lot easier on him than on ours. He'd only been married for just a few years; it's easier when there's not much of a past...

Of course, I wish it had been no one at all and that this nightmare had never happened, but I can't help but think how it would be easier, less painful, if it had been one of the other officers...

I have to be honest; I can't help but wish that it had been...
That makes me awful, I know.
What kind of person wishes this pain on another?
I don't wish this pain on even my worst enemies.. but I can't help but have these thoughts... these wishes...

Memories

Memories don't always last forever.
They simply cannot.
Our brains just can't keep everything in.
The longer time passes, the harder it is to remember things.
Incidental happenings, minor moments, simple passings...they fade away.

It's the big things you often remember.
It's the important things you try desperately to hold onto.
The special times.
The problem is you don't know what is truly special enough to hold onto,
and you don't know when the day will come that you wish you had captured every moment that you could have.
By then, it's too late.

You just have to try and take in everything that you can. Write things down. Take photos, videos.
Think about the moments regularly and make them permanent. As permanent as possible at least.
Until one day when your brain just turns to mush and everything is gone.

I don't remember my dad at all, and most of my memories of my mom are nearly gone as well.

I don't want that for my kids. I don't want them to wake up one day, and he's gone.

He's already gone enough.
Memories are all we have.
But memories don't last forever.

But love does. And that has to be enough.

Crazy, Mad, Stupid

Grief makes you crazy.

Seeing things, hearing things, thoughts that invade your soul. Thinking he will call, text, be home any minute. It's all a bad dream, a prank, a mistake. He's still out there, coming home soon. You feel frozen in time, but time moves forward, yet you feel stuck. Stuck in the what ifs and should bes, the memories and lost dreams. The regrets take control. Like a darkness. A plague. Lonely even when you're not alone.

Grief makes you mad.

Angry, fuming, heated. Pierced lips, clenched fists, hate fills your mind, fuels your body and you scream and just want to hit, throw, hurt. Enraged with pain. Breaking and broken and you can't understand why the world doesn't crumble with you, yet it feels as if it is falling apart and laying in a pile of tears and emptiness.

Grief makes you stupid.

Crying out, screaming, begging for them to come back. Knowing that's not possible yet feeling as if it could still really happen. Maybe if you yell loud enough. Maybe if you beg and barter with God enough. Maybe if you make the right promise. If you say the right thing, do the right thing, maybe.

I Dream of You

In the silence of the night, I pretend I can still hear your heartbeat beside me.

In the cold emptiness I reach out and imagine your warm embrace.

In the lonely hours I envision your eyes gazed upon me.

In the quiet despair of the moon, I close my eyes and dream of you.

Easier and Better

It's better because they didn't have kids.
It's easier because their kids are younger and don't understand and won't remember.
It's easier because their kids are older and can manage without.

It's better because they weren't married. They can find someone else.
It's easier because they weren't married very long and don't have many memories yet.
It's better because they were married a long time and had already spent enough time together.

It's easier because they had been sick a long time. They had time to say goodbye.
It's better because it happened suddenly. They didn't suffer.

It's better because they have insurance, and they'll get money.
It's easier because they didn't have much so no one will fight over stuff.

It's easier because they had a big family so there's lots of support.
It's better because they didn't have any family so there's no one left behind.

It's easier because they were old. They lived a long life.
It's better because they were young. They didn't have to grow old.

It gets easier with time.
Things will get better. Give it time.

Easier.
Better.
Easier.
Better.

It will never get easier.

It will never be better.

For a Moment

I sat in the old soda fountain the other day to grab a quick lunch.
At the counter sat an elderly couple.
As they stood to leave, the gentlemen helped his bride step down.
He sweetly caressed her arm and slid his hand along her back.
After all those years the love was still apparent in that simple gesture.

I fought back the tears as I replaced them with an image of us in their place.
An image of what should have been.
I imagined for a moment our love would still be so strong as well after all those years.
I imagined the feeling of your hand upon my back. The gentle touch of your fingers down my spine.
I imagined being old but still hot for each other.

I imagined for a moment what should have been.

Lost in Thought

"Earth to mother...come back in...mom, can you hear me...are you OK?
Oh, sorry, just lost in thought, I guess.

Horns begin blaring-red light has turned green...
Oh, sorry, just lost in thought, I guess.

Instinctively turn the page, then realize I haven't actually read anything prior...
the movie is several scenes in, and I have no idea what's happening...
Oh, sorry, just lost in thought, I guess.

The shower turns cold-several minutes have passed and the water is no longer hot.
Once again, I've been lost in thought.

The pot overflows in the sink...the ground is drenched beneath the rose into a puddle from the water hose...

Sometimes it's just a word, an image that brings back a memory, a song, a moment, a smell, a sound,
seeing someone from across the room that reminds me of you,
seeing something that makes me wish it were you....
and suddenly I am transported through time,
taken away, captured and held hostage within my imagination,
replaying scenes from our lives,
wishing the past were the present,
fantasizing,
pretending you are there...

You know, truth is, I'm not really sorry when I'm lost in thought,
for in that moment,
you are here, and all is well, all is back to how it should be...
so let me get lost in thought-
my thoughts are all I have now.

Forever 37, Forever 18 Years

Do you ever just feel stuck, stagnant, like the world is moving around you while you stand still in the center?

The sun rises and sets, the moon pulls the tides each day, and you know time keeps ticking, yet the clock is silent.

You look in the mirror and see the wrinkles slowly appearing, the grey hairs keep coming,
but everything around you seems to be frozen.

I feel like my purpose in life is no more.
My husband is gone - my house doesn't feel like a home anymore.
My kids are grown - they don't really need me much anymore.
I don't see the walls of a classroom being my refuge anymore.
I don't know where I fit in anymore.

My days are simply routine.
Auto-pilot switches on and I just sort of float around, skimming the surface of life.
I breathe, my heart beats, my dna is etched within the atmosphere, I exist, but I don't live.
I just simply am.

Maybe it's more accurate to say I just simply were.
I don't feel like I am.

I long to be but don't know if my was and will and could be can even come together.

I'm a pool of contradictions. I want to but don't have the motivation. I wish but don't apply.
I hope but faith is withered. I need a reset.
I need an awakening, a renewal but how can I imagine a future with no you.

How can I move forward with the world when my world has crumbled.

How can the world keep turning when I don't know how to turn with it.

I Wish People Knew

I wish people knew how many nights I sat in bed, drenched in tears, wishing I had someone to talk to, to help distract my mind, calm me down, and tell me it's OK.

I wish people knew how many times I had to catch my breath, secretly wipe away my eyes, and choke back the cries as I sat alone at the kids' events.

I wish people knew watching Mark play basketball alone, start shaving, struggle to tie a tie, having to do all the house stuff on his own, and everything a dad should be there for made me wish it had been me instead.

I wish people knew how many times I wanted desperately to be alone to scream in despair, yet fearfully aware of the loneliness that waited for me each night and day, and as the kids all moved away and desperately wishing I had friends nearby.

I wish people knew that each time I posted a message or photo, it was my attempt to ensure you were never forgotten and secretly hope that someone would reach out and check on me.

I wish people knew how many times I didn't post something because I knew people were probably annoyed that I posted so much.

I wish people knew that I knew they stopped following my pages because of that.

I wish people knew how important it is that they share things about you, talk about you, ask about the kids, and remember you.

I wish people knew that the kids stuffed all their tears inside and looked like they were OK, even though home was very different than what everyone saw.

I wish people knew that the thought of putting all your things away made me physically ill, and I couldn't force myself to even throw away your empty water bottle on the table.

I wish people knew that every time they asked me how we were doing, it made me want to scream and tell them how much I hate each day.

I wish people knew that my days were filled with intrusive thoughts, and sometimes I wished it would all just be over, and we could be together again.

I wish people knew that I really, really needed help, but people either gave me a recommendation on who to call, told me to watch YouTube, or just said they were sorry things are so tough.

I wish people knew I could have done that myself without asking but I was so beyond exhausted from always having to do everything on my own and I just wished once someone would offer to do it for me.

I wish people knew how hard every single day was, and how I couldn't stand the thought of having to endure years and decades until we could be together again.

People knew I was sad, but I wish people knew, truly knew.

Things you're not prepared for in grief:

1. grocery shopping and having to adjust what you buy, how much you buy, and seeing things he would've wanted-

2. going to your kids' events alone and seeing the other families there or seeing kids without dads there knowing that your kids' dad would have been there-

3. restaurants on a Friday night and people on dates-

4. places for family fun when your family is missing one-

5. when someone else dies-

6. when someone gets their miracle, a cure, survives, lives-

7. people getting married, celebrating anniversaries-

8. hearing your daughter say, "hello husband" to her husband when he comes home from work but yours never will and you will never say hello to yours ever again-

9. listening to someone complain about their spouse, talk badly about their spouse, gripe, nag, belittle, or simply be unappreciative of their spouse-

10. listening to people go on and on about how hard things are for them when it's so not a big deal and you really want to punch them and tell them to get over it-

11. the Tik tok filter trend showing couples and what they will look like when they are old-

Oh, so many other things you're not prepared for...

Too many to name...too many unknown, but when they happen, you will know...but you won't be prepared...

What not to say to a widow or really anyone in grief:

He/She's in a better place now.
(He should be here with us.)

There's a reason for everything.
(There's no reason for us to have to suffer like this.)

God has a plan. Trust His plan.
(Not really helpful…)

When are you going to start dating again or will you ever remarry?
(Are you kidding me?!?)
(Had this happen less than two months after my husband died.)

I understand…when my cat died….
(Just smile and nod…and bite your tongue.)

I'm sorry I haven't called… I didn't want to bother you.
(So instead you let me be alone and forgotten…?)

I didn't want to say anything to make you sad.
(I'm always sad - talking about my husband means he is still remembered.)

I'll pray for you.
(Thanks, but I prayed my husband would be ok. Prayers don't really help me right now.)

At least you'll get social security for the kids/did he have a good insurance policy?
(Just smile and nod…and bite your tongue.
I would give back every single penny, go into foreclosure,
have every belonging repossessed, sold off, taken away, live on the streets if it meant I could have my husband
back.)

Call me if you need anything.
(Find a need…I'm not going to call…I need everything but really I need my husband and no-one can help there.)

There's really nothing good to say…so just don't try and say anything – just hug and show up.

A love letter from those who have passed on...

Take the love you have for me
And radiate it outwards
Allowing it to touch and impact others

Take the memory you have of me
And use it as a source of inspiration
To live fully, meaningfully and intentionally

Take the image you have of me in your mind
And allow it to fuel you
To take action
Seize the day
And be reminded of what is most important in life

Take the care you have for me
And let it remind you
To care for yourself fully
And shower yourself with your own love

And take the pain and grief you feel
Following my loss
And alchemize it into
Love, compassion and beauty

Build a castle
From the wreckage of my passing
And allow it to unlock your greatness and potential
And empower you to become more than you ever thought you were capable of being

And know that I can never truly leave you
And will always remain beside you
Watching over you in spirit
And that the love I have for you lives on
Through the connections you form
The kindness and compassion you share
And the future relationships and friendships you cultivate.

And until we are one day reunited
I will remain with you
Through the storms and chaos of life

And am always beside you
Walking with you, laughing with you, crying with you and smiling with you

And I am proud of you for being strong
I am proud of you for being brave
And I am proud of you for being you.

Words by Tahlia Hunter

Up There

I bet you're up there,
Making lots of jokes.
I bet you're up there,
Loving the music I know.
I bet you're up there,
And it's so beautiful now;
But you're sure awfully missed down here on the ground.

The reason, the purpose, the why, or God's plan- none of it makes sense;
Nothing will explain why we have to endure this pain - it's just too intense.
No words make it better, nothing anyone can say or do,
The absence of your presence is so blatantly true.
I try to tell myself that you're waiting for me,
and I imagine that day and how it will be and I -

I bet you're up there,
Making lots of jokes.
I bet you're up there,
Loving the music I know.
I bet you're up there,
And it's so beautiful now;
But you're sure awfully missed down here on the ground.

I wish we could rewind the gears,
I wish the clock could go back so many years.
I wish you were here and this was all just a bad dream,
If we could just wake up and go back to how it should be.
I know that's not so, not the way it can go,
So I just look up into the skies, close my eyes and I know-

I know you're up there,
Making lots of jokes.
I know you're up there,
Loving the music I know.
I know you're up there,
And it's so beautiful now;
But you're sure awfully missed down here on the ground.

You're sure awfully missed ----
down here on the ground.

Things you've missed so far:

Work. Ugh. I don't know what to do. I quit teaching. It's just too much, but I'm awfully lonely during the day. I need to do something. Money is ok, but I really should do something.

Changed some things at the house. You would like it all. But there's still so much needed and I don't know what to do about some things. Had a hurricane and two freezes cause tons of damage. I tried so hard to fix everything.

New pets. Monkey is a sweet kitty. You would really like Picasso. Chap has been good for me. The guinea pigs died. Cheeto died. Lucy got attacked by Miley. She's ok but got nasty dealing with the neighbors over it. I hate dealing with them now.

The new annex named in your honor (your beautiful name in big letters for all to see and all to know and wonder and seek to know), your Honor chair in your academy for all to see and know and seek to know, your name forever etched in stone in DC, Austin, FBCSO, and the APHoF memorial walls, the Running for Heroes Tribute Hall, and so amazing of them all - the Caleb Rule law...

You missed seeing the kids' dance, sports, and performances – you rarely missed a game and said you would drive an hour just to watch them sit the bench – you hated missing things.

Birthdays – they're getting so big...so beautiful...

Lizzie has been amazing in theatre. You would be beaming watching her on stage and don't get me started on music – she is 1st chair in the top band and is working towards making it to state. She also made drum major for next year! I know you would be over the moon to carry her podium and watch her conduct.

Kids all got their drivers licenses and cars. You would've been better at teaching them. It took them all a few months longer than it should and Lizzie three tries at the test. I got them all cars, but Mark's broke down within a year. I don't know what I'm doing, baby. I'm not good at this stuff.

My gallbladder surgery – finally went to the ER - and my wreck. I really needed you. I know you were there protecting me, you had to have been – that wreck was really bad.

Trips. Feel guilty about going without you.

Kid's graduations. You should've been there.

Annie and the army. She cut off all her hair! She is a Military Police Officer now.

Colleges. Our babies are growing up...in two more years, they will all be moved out and I will truly be alone.

Annie's wedding. It was beautiful...three more to go – and you will miss them all as well.

The Baby. I don't even know what to say. She is beautiful and you would love being Pops. I don't even know what you would have wanted to be called. She is such a blessing to our family, and I can't help but think you sent her to us.

You've missed everything and will continue to miss everything, and it isn't fair. You should be here.

Unfilled Photo Albums

Finished filling all the photo albums today.
I've printed out every photo of you that I have - even screenshots of conversations, Facebook posts, and photos you took.
Sunsets, the sky, nature, and the beauty of nature through your eyes.
You throughout the years, with the kids, with me, at work, on trips, special times, moments with family and friends.
Everything has been put into frames around the house and in photo albums sitting on the shelf.

Every photo.
Every memory.
Every moment with you.

That's it.
There isn't anymore.

Reached the end of the photo album, yet there were still pages left...and the pages will never be filled.

That's it.
There isn't anymore.

We will forever have unfilled photo albums.

To Do List

There are quite a few things around the house that need to be done, taken care of, fixed, and such.
There are quite a few things I need help with and can't do on my own or don't know how to do.
I know people are busy and can't always come help me do things though...

> ...So the things haven't been done.

I know I can probably figure out how to do most or even all of them on my own.
I'm sure there is a YouTube video, a TikTok, or online manual somewhere.
I'm sure I can call someone and have them explain or text me instructions...

> ...But dammit, I shouldn't have to do that.

Someone should come help me.
I shouldn't have to do everything on my own.
Someone should step up and stand in for Caleb.
I shouldn't even have to ask.
Someone should be here.
Caleb should be here.

The Radio

80s rock that makes me smile, remembering you singing along.
Your alarm. The high notes. Drumming on the steering wheel.
Rock of Ages making me move. Move in closer. A grin and a nod.
Country songs from date nights and dancing.
Laughing but loving every moment, even if it was off rhythm.
The Neon Moon pulling me in. Lonely but not the same.
The Dance - the pain, oh but having to miss the dance would hurt so much more.
Tomorrow never came. I hope you know.
Driving by each other on the way home.
Texts with the station.
Hurry. Change the channel. Sending a message.
Your guitar, piano, making up tunes.
Songs for me. Giving it all up for me.
Play again. Play all you want.
The silence from the gathering dust is so loud.
Rascal Flatts and Changed. Changed for the good. Take me back.
Taylors songs, breakups and broken hearts – nothing comes close to the broken heart I feel.
Reba and the end of the road, and the mountain, and the ocean.
Somehow. I'm trying. Every day.
Luke had it right, Some Things Last Forever.
Infinite love. John 16:22.
Luna, Mayonnaise, Melancholy, and more. Knowing everything about them.
The concert double trip and secret love.
Wicked and other showtunes. Eye rolls and smiles. My perfect match.
Sinatra and Christmas and Charlie Brown and cooking.
Should have danced in the kitchen.
Turn it back on. Turn it up.
I would give anything to hear hey google again.
Your playlist plays forevermore.
Your crazy playlist. Never know what you'll get.
But no matter what, they all lead to you.
So many memories. So many reminders.
Tears and tears. Smiles, sways, and more tears.
When I miss you, when I need you, when I want you near...
I find you on the radio.

Grief is tricky.
It doesn't really go away.
We always carry it.
It's kind of like having on a backpack that can't be taken off.
Sometimes it is so light, I almost forget I have it on –
I can even pull out a little memory with a smile.
But other times, like holidays or even when a certain song comes on,
it feels like someone has filled it with rocks.
It's so heavy I don't understand how I can move forward.
But somehow, I do.

-Hannah Dearth

Everyone's grief is different.
We may share the same losses,
but not the same grief.
Grief is composed of pain,
but also from our beliefs, traumas, personality
and relationship with whom we carry in our hearts.
What works for one may not for another.
Be gentle with yourself and with others.

-Author Unknown

Pulling Me In

In the clear of the skies, I can see your eyes.
Arctic blue with sapphire hues piercing my soul like a peaceful winter breeze.
The warmth of your smile like the country sunset bringing hope to the end of the worries of a summer day.
A smirk, a grin, a wink, the look in your eye and I love yous across the room.
The safety of your eyes, intoxicating glance, looking just beneath and within.
The clouds look down and I see you staring back, pulling me in.

In the glimmer of the stars, I can feel your presence and we're no longer apart.
The silence of the night, the crisp satin mist, encircles me and holds me in.
The breathtaking comfort of your embrace like the blaze of the moon bringing life to the darkness of the still night.
I close my eyes and breathe you in.
The safety of your arms, intoxicating grasp, fitting just beneath and within.
The stars look down and I feel you reaching out, pulling me in.

Look down, reach out.
Pull me in and never look away.
Pull me in and never let go.
Clear, blue skies.
Star filled, moonlit nights.
Pulling me in.

If I Had Known

If I had known, would I have run, hopped on a train,
so I'd avoid the pain and my heartache would be none.
Would I have missed out on all the love and joy if I had known.

Would I have skipped all those years,
so I would never have had all these tears and never felt this emptiness.
Would I have never felt your gentle touch, your embrace, your kiss if I had known.

If I had known, would I have looked the other way, found someone else,
never have shared the bench that day.
Would I have never had your name, this life, our beautiful kids if I had known.

If I had known I could have rewound the clock, made it stop, or moved time forward.
If I had known I could have done it all differently,
but different it would be, and then it may not have been you and me.

If I had known...
the only thing I would have changed would have been to pull you closer, sooner, longer.

Final Entry but Not the Finale

This is my final entry,
but it's not the finale by any means.
My love will never end,
therefore, neither will my grief.
I am not cured, healed, fixed, or better - only changed.
Changed in ways I can't always explain.
I see the world differently now.
A raindrop is not just a raindrop anymore.
A newly sprouted flower not just a flower.
A cloud, a sunset, a windmill, a wave...
I feel differently, I love differently, I even breathe differently.
I am not the same me that I was.
My love for you isn't even the same anymore -
and that hurts.
I should've loved you more when I had the chance.
Someday I will make it up to you,
when someday comes.
Until then, the journey continues,
this is not the end.
There is no finish line to cross or bell to ring.
There is nothing to indicate my journey is complete.
I could fill a hundred more pages, maybe even a thousand.
I have so much more to say, so many more stories.
My heart is full, overflowing with emotions.
Ever changing but never ending.
I may be writing my last entry for this collection,
but it's not the last of me.
I will keep on,
keep on getting out of bed each day,
keep on putting one foot in front of the other each day,
keep saying your name each day,
keep thinking about you, longing for you, missing you each day,
keep going to bed without you each day.
But one more day without you is another day closer to being with you again.
Then and there my finish line awaits.

Annie

Our first.
Our biggest baby girl.
The one who started it all.
Who made us a family - a mommy, a daddy, a little girl.
Who kept us together despite their attempts to break us apart.
The phone to my belly, come home every weekend, final exams, pack and hurry home, pillow, backpack in hand, just in time.
Hold me tight, will she be okay, that look in the window, the worry, the fear.
The joy, all worth it, so much love, immediate connection, your smile, give me my daughter.
A real family. Forever.
Every morning til night.
Until no more goodnight goodbyes -
you should get married, let's get married, you should get married, we're getting married.
A real family. Forever.
Our first.
First of everything and made us want more.
First experiences, first milestones.
Until the last day – the first of big plans to come.
Excitement awaits, house is ready, plan for the weekend.
It was her big day, first real big girl big day, first of many...
But not the way we planned.
Tears of joy with little joy.
You would have been so proud.

Should have seen how she held her head high...
even with her head down so low.
She kept going...army, college, married, and a mommy now.
You would have loved her letters, her calls, her stories.
Would be better at giving her direction.
She changed her plans - life changed her plans.
Our biggest baby girl.
Stubborn, strong willed, fierce, loud, eye rolls, brick wall,
passionate, emotional, all of the above.
Looks just like me with brains just like you...
not always a compliment...just kidding.
Makes me smile, makes me cry, makes me crazy.
By my side though it all - because of missing you...
even while missing you.
Many more firsts but your last.
Our biggest baby girl with our first baby girl -
Just missing you.
Thank you for giving me her and you and...her now, too.
Our biggest baby girl.

Rosalan

Our spitfire, red like the flames, wild one.
Attitude and personality to match, as expected.
Eyes like the peaceful woodland queen.
Stunning, brilliant, gentle.
Heart of gold.
Little lady with a wild bite.
Loves like you, feels deeply like you,
hurts like you.
Some of me, but mostly you.
The two of you always clicked.
You understood her,
You mended her.
Who will put the pieces back together now?
Our beautiful little girl.
Our squirrel.
"Warm heart, cold noses."
"No, Daddy."
"It's the circus."
Kicking her toe...stubborn.
So many silly stories.
Such a sweet little girl.
Such a delicate little lady.
Such a hopeful young woman.
So much more to do, to live, to learn, to be.
Missing you.
Missing a part of herself.
Missing you.
Your jokes, your thoughts, your wit, and grin.
A piece of you.
Sometimes I wish she was more of me,
and then I see she is so much of you.
Our beautiful little girl.
Our Razi Roo.

Mark

Three of four but the first, the only.
Our little boy.
Your buddy.
Rub my feet, growing pains, run your fingers through my hair.
Baseball, football, basketball, legos, cars, outdoors, and more.
Shoot hoops, fishing, little wranglers first prize burgers and pork chops, yard work, boy stuff.
Just the guys.
Sweet boy, gentleman, so much like his dad.
Loud, silly, jokes, and laughs like you.
Had a good role model.
Knows how to be a good man.
Just missed out on how to do lots of things like a man.
Cheated. Stolen. Taken.
Right when he needed a man.
Right when he needed his dad.
Moms just can't do some things.
Moms just shouldn't do some things.
I can't do some things.
He needs his dad.
He wants his dad.
Tools and sports and shaving and suits and ties.
Boy stuff. Man stuff.
He needs his dad.
He wants his dad. He doesn't want his mom.
Anger. Pain. Fears. Battles.
Tried so hard.
Couldn't look. Didn't cry. Buried it.
Pushed it aside. Hidden. Pretending.
Young man.
Young boy still.
Be a man.
Must. Have to. No choice.
Man of the house now.
No one else can do some things.
Trying.
Making you proud.
Grown so much. Changed so much.
But still our little boy.
Much bigger than both of us;
he's way taller than you now,
but always our little boy.
Always, your Buddy.

DANGEROUS AREA
DO NOT CROSS FENCE

Lizzie

The one who completed our family.
Made us whole.
The ending we never knew we needed.
A surprise that brought total joy.
A happily ever after.
Your Pooks, Pookie, Pinkie Pie, Lou.
Silly little girl.
Makes me smile.
Your twin.
Makes me cry.
I see you.
She was just a young girl.
Still needing her daddy.
Not quite to dad yet... still daddy.
Just starting to become who she would be.
Now the she that she is may not be the she
she would have been.
The she you will never know.
Will she be able to remember like the others?
Only a couple years separates,
but could it have been the difference.
Will I be able to remind her enough?
Will I be able to finish raising her on my own?
Will I be able to help her be the she
she was meant to be even without you?
Little girl, now a young lady.
You're missing her becoming a young woman.
Beautiful young woman.
Missing all her greats.
Music like you.
Funny like you.
Gentle like you.
Loving like you.
Your twin.
Your Pooks, Pookie, Pinkie Pie, Lou.

Scarlett Luna

Our first grandbaby.
The first of which you will never know, yet I like to think you already met.
Handpicked. Specifically chosen by you.
In the Heavens, you sought her out, you knew she would be the perfect choice from the angels to be sent to us, to me, to give new purpose, new drive, new life, new reason to keep pushing forward.
Her smile has reunited me with joy, reminded me of how to feel hope.
Her eyes shine like yours and when I hold her close, I sometimes feel you whispering within my soul.
Eyes like the sky, the ocean, the beauty of the world of love.
Your love which makes me whole.
She looks at your photos and admires them with a sense of remembrance.
She reaches for you as if she remembers how it felt to be held in your arms.
A feeling I know so closely, so deeply. A feeling I miss more than my tears can express.
As she grows, and learns, and lives, you too will live, for we will all tell her about her Pops.
She will know about the man you were and always will be.
As she walks through life, I know you will be standing close, right beside her, watching her, guiding her, keeping her safe.
And as our babies bring us more grandbabies in the years to come, I can breathe with ease knowing they will all move mountains –
for they will all hold your strength, your passion, your gentleness.
They will all hold you.

Our last family photo taken five months before Caleb was killed.

My father died in 1991, at the age of 29. He went to work that morning, worked a double shift to get some extra funds, went to the company softball tournament that evening, and then stopped by a friend's house on the way home...but he never made it home. He was found in the middle of the night after his car drove off the roadway, through a guardrail, off a bridge, and crashed on the roadway next to the Brazos River. We can only assume he fell asleep. He was life flighted to the nearest trauma hospital, but his injuries were too severe. My mom woke up the next morning having no idea where he was and began frantically calling his co-workers and local hospitals. She didn't locate him until later that day. I was seven years old, and my brother was only 18 months old. We don't really remember anything about him or much about the years to follow. My mom remarried quickly and pretty much tried to mask her grief for our sake. We never talked about my dad often and after a few years, rarely at all, unless I asked a question about him. My mother and her second husband were married for eight years before he met another woman and moved out...sending my mother into a spiraling and dark depression that would eventually lead to her death. In the fall of 2000, a month after my 17th birthday and only a few weeks into my senior year, my mother surrendered to her demons and took her life. I was the one who found her body and had to notify 911 and our family. I have tried to make sure that her memory remains for my brother and my little sister; however, my sister went to live with her dad and his new wife, and they pretty much erased my mother's existence under the excuse of not wanting my sister to be sad. I went to live with my aunt and didn't get to see my sister much until she was older. She and I are very close now. Our brother struggled through the years, having trouble in school and with authority, masking his pain with drugs. He and I barely talk anymore. I tried so hard to help him in those initial years after our mother's death, but I was only a kid myself. I didn't know how to grieve on my own, much less help an 11-year-old grieve. Fortunately, I had my friends and the resiliency of being a teenager to help me. I finished high school with honors and married soon after graduation. I thought the days of tragedy and trauma were behind me when I formed a family of my own; however, my parents' deaths were just the beginning.

On May 29, 2020, my life was completely shattered. Flipped upside down. Halted. Broken. Destroyed.

My friend of 25 years, true love of 20 years, and husband of 18 years was shot and killed in the line of duty. The father of my four children. My soulmate. My everything. This is not how my life was supposed to be and, at that moment, nothing made sense. Nothing was okay. Nothing brought me hope. Many people offered support the best and only ways they could, but I needed my husband, and no one could make that happen. Everything I knew and trusted and believed was gone. So many plans and hopes and dreams, gone. All that was left were tears, anger, regrets, and fear. One of the heaviest feats of his death has been the terrible reality that after our children and I are gone, there will be no one left to remember him. To honor him. To think of him. To say his name. He will never meet his grandchildren and never be able to pass on his infectious energy, love, and compassion. My worst fear is he will be forgotten.

Caleb Daniel Rule was born June 5, 1982, in Salina, Kansas. His family moved to Houston, Texas when he was a young boy, then made their home in Needville, Texas as he entered middle school. His father pastored a local church, and his mother was a teacher, so they quickly became very involved in the community. Caleb was also involved in several activities throughout school. He was an extremely talented musician, playing just about every instrument by ear and loved sports. He also found an interest in theatre and photography later in life. Caleb was known for being extremely social - making friends with anyone he met - and talking your ear off about any topic that came about. He was knowledgeable on every subject and often referred to as a "human Wikipedia." He knew just about any movie quote and was always prepared with a joke, one-liner, or witty comment. Caleb was known as "Work Dad." He was the officer you wanted on scene as he was confident, knowledgeable, and compassionate. He wholly represented the slogan, "I've got your six" and was always the first to check by. He served the badge with dignity and was constantly giving out advice and assistance to anyone. So many people have reached out to share stories of how Caleb impacted their lives - fellow officers, past friends, victims, and even former suspects and criminals.

Caleb and I met in 7th grade; we both played trumpet and shared a few other classes as well. We weren't really friends at first though. I thought Caleb was arrogant and cocky (mainly because he was so good at trumpet and seemed to always show off - I realized later it was because he loved music so much). One time in math class, Caleb was cheating on a test, and I told the teacher... Caleb then said some pretty mean words to me, so I told on him again! Of course, we forgave each other and had lots of laughs about it years later. It wasn't until high school that we began to like each other. One day in 10th grade, I was waiting for my mom, who was also a police officer, to pick me up from the basketball game after school; Caleb waited with me because my mom had a last-minute call and was running late. We sat together waiting for a few minutes and slowly formed a friendship thereafter, which turned romantic in our senior year, and the rest is history! We graduated together in May of 2001, were engaged in August, and married April 6, 2002. We celebrated 18 years of marriage the month before Caleb was killed. We have four beautiful children - Annie, Rosalan, Mark, and Lizzie. Annie graduated high school the day Caleb was killed and is currently a student at Texas State University. She is pursuing her Master's Degree to be an Occupational Therapy Assistant. She has her dad's passion for community and is a Military Police Officer with the Texas Army National Guard. She is partly responsible for the new change in Texas LODD educational benefits known as the Caleb Rule Law which extended benefits to dependent children 18-25. She was married in 2022 and had our first grandbaby, Scarlett Luna, in January of 2023. Rosalan attends the University of Texas at San Antonio and is majoring in education; she has her dad's weird sense of humor and generous, fiery spirit. Mark is attending the local junior college and has an interest in biology - he gets that from his dad. He has recently been thinking about becoming a game warden; I don't know how I feel about that, but I am beyond proud of him. He has probably struggled the most, missing school, lashing out, and so forth. I struggle the most with him personally because I don't know how to relate to a teenage boy - he needs his dad. Lizzie is still in high school where she is drum major and section leader in band and part of the school's theatre company. She shares her father's passion and talent in music. She hopes to pursue music as a career. She reminds me the most of Caleb.

Caleb loved being a police officer and had even considered pursuing a career with the FBI. He began his career in law enforcement in 2001, as a campus guard with the Sam Houston State University Police Department. In 2002, he began working in dispatch at Rosenberg Police Department, then became a Correctional Officer for the Fort Bend County Sheriff's Office, where he attended the Gus George Law Enforcement Academy and graduated in June of 2004. He continued to work as a deputy in the jail until he was offered a patrol position with the Missouri City Police Department in December of 2004. He was employed with MCPD for over 14 years, working his way through various divisions such as: Dive Team, Bike Patrol, the Burglary and Auto Theft Task Force, and CID. He was also an Instructor and Field Training Officer. He was very proud to be an Investigator with the BAT Team and enjoyed meeting people throughout the state. He left MCPD in 2018, worked in Private Investigations for a few months, and then began the last leg of his LEO career with the Fort Bend County Precinct 4 Constable's Office, where he was contracted to patrol the Riverstone subdivision in Missouri City. He enjoyed working for Precinct 4. He really liked being a mentor to the younger and less experienced officers in the small agency and being able to share the knowledge he brought with him from 14 years in a big city. He served as a Deputy Constable with precinct 4 for almost a year before being tragically killed in the line of duty while assisting the FBCSO on a suspicious person call. On May 29, 2020, at 1:45am, Caleb and three deputies responded to a call of a "suspicious person running down the street and possibly entering the backyard of a vacant house." As they were finishing searching the home, one of the deputies "mistook Caleb as a possible intruder" as he exited one of the rooms; the deputy discharged his weapon at Caleb, fatally shooting him in the shoulder. The officer took a plea out of court and surrendered his police license. I can only hope this horrible act of carelessness can help bring change through better training opportunities, equipment, and procedures - not to mention teach rookie officers how to handle themselves during similar situations. If anything, it will be an opportunity for officers to know Caleb's name.

Three years later, I am still taking life one day at a time, struggling, but trying to do the best I can to keep things going for our children. I was a theatre teacher but had to quit working to be available for the kids, the countless meetings and appointments that come along with a line of duty death, and my own mental health; I don't know if or when I will go back to work full time. I am still involved in local community theatre though and teach musical theatre camps during the summer and winter holidays at a nearby dance studio. I write poetry to cope and enjoy various activities and trips with the kids. Being a solo parent is hard, but the kids keep me busy and distracted, especially our new grandbaby. When the kids and I are not busy with school activities, we can be found doing whatever we can to keep Caleb's memory and legacy alive. Not a day goes by that Caleb isn't talked about, remembered, honored, and sorely missed. There is a law named in his honor, he has an Honor Chair at the police academy he attended, and one of the county public safety annexes is named in his honor; his name is forever etched in stone on the Fort Bend County, Texas state, and Washington, D.C. national memorial monuments, as well as the American Police Hall of Fame memorial and the Running 4 Heroes Tribute Hall, both located in Florida. Our high school also has a memorial bench with his name and picture on display outside the band hall. Caleb will never be forgotten - a hero remembered never dies. Caleb was one of the good ones, maybe even the best ones, and the world will never be the same without his energy and love. I will never be the same, but I am facing my grief journey head on. I hope that my poems and stories do the same for you. If anything, I hope you can relate and know that we are on this journey together...today and always.

Here are a few poems I wrote years ago while Caleb and I were dating and a few during marriage; there are even a couple poems he wrote to me. I thought it would be nice to add them here as well; although they are not about grief, they are still a part of Caleb and my story. I hope you like them. I think I have grown quite a bit as a writer since these. They are a bit cheesy, but that's what love does to you!

June 17, 2001
(Caleb's parents wanted us to break up at one point in our relationship; I wrote this poem to let him know that no matter what may come between us, we were meant to be.)

You've impacted my heart and imprinted my mind,
when I envision my future, you're all I find.
If I had one wish, I'd turn to you,
then and only then, all my skies would be blue.
My sun would shine brighter, and the rains would all fade,
my heart would be mended, you'd come to my aide.
It's not by coincidence we've come to be,
I believe in fate, perhaps it's destiny.
If that is true, all the things will work out,
we'll end up forever, there is no doubt.
These things I believe straight from my heart,
I'll dream of you when we're apart.
I'll go my own way and you'll go yours,
just remember for always I live with open doors.
With compassion and true forgiveness,
things will come together,
our love will be shared, and we will be forever.
I guess for now it's not meant to be,
but maybe through time, God willingly.

High School Senior Trip

The summer after senior year.

June 26, 2001
(His parents quickly realized they couldn't keep us apart!)

Prayers are possible, faith is true,
by not giving up hope, I am with you.
I never gave up that we would be,
I always believed in you and me.
From this day forward my happiness prevails,
only unto you my love unveils.
My hand in yours, your arms around me,
I feel total comfort and immense safety.
A perfect picture of love so true,
our hearts are connected and will never undo.

October 2001
There's Something Special in You

There's a safety in your arms that takes away my fears;
There's a comfort in your smile that remains through all the years.
You have a spirit of true forgiveness and a heart full of generosity;
I can wake each morning content for the love you've shared with me.
All of my worries fade away from the passion in your kiss,
that sparkle in your baby blues is something I never want to miss.
I thank my lucky stars for everything you have within;
God so graciously brought you to me, and I am forever grateful unto Him.
I don't know how our life will be, but I know we'll be together.
I know in my heart we're meant to be, and our love will last forever.
I thought I had all the answers and knew you all throughout,
but I've discovered something new – there's something I can't figure out.
I'm not certain what it is, but I know it exists and is true.
I can only sum it up in just one way, there's something special in you.
Maybe one day it will become clear, the mystery will be solved and through,
but until then all I know is there's something special in you.

August 22, 2001
(Caleb wrote this for me as part of his proposal. He took me to dinner for my birthday and afterwards, he handed me the ring and said, "I originally bought this to be a promise ring, but now I know I want it to mean much more. Eden, will you marry me? Of course, I said, "Yes!")

> With this ring comes a promise of my love to you,
> a love as strong as life itself,
> my love's completely true.
> A perfect golden circle represents eternity,
> when I hear the word forever,
> I think of you and me.
> A promise of my love so true,
> I'll hold you in my heart and think of you every day,
> every moment we're apart,
> and even in the darkest hour I'll hold you close all night,
> to kiss your lips and hold your hands,
> everything will be alright.
> Our love will last forever,
> that is not simply a guess,
> God has given us unending love and eternal happiness.

February 14, 2020
(Caleb wrote this in lipstick on my bathroom mirror and gave me a vase full of flowers for Valentines Day 2020. I still have this poem written on my mirror; I will never wash it off.)

> A single pretty flower
> will brighten up your day,
> so here are lots of flowers
> to show you every way,
> that every moment spent with you,
> and every word you say,
> and every time you smile,
> it takes my breath away.
> For every moment that we've shared
> as husband and wife,
> I could never thank you enough
> for being in my life.

There were many more poems between the two of us throughout the years, but these were just a few I wanted to include in this collection. I feel they sum up our love story very well. We had a love so strong, so real, so deep...it's no wonder my grief is so heavy. The greatest love bears the greatest grief.

My Dad and Mom shortly before I was born.

Printed in the USA
CPSIA information can be obtained
at www.ICGtesting.com
LVHW061948061223
765353LV00074B/1460

9 781662 945267